"A street corner preacher at twenty-five, ... journey to discover his authentic self, and offers us s ... inspiring stories to help us do the same. Clearly, assisting people i... removing the blocks that keep them from their authentic self is his true calling—this book is a generous toolbox of support." **August Gold**

Finding
Authentic You

Concise Version with 50 Daily Discoveries

BO SEBASTIAN

Copyright © 2016 Finding Authentic You Publishing

All rights reserved.

This book may contain references to situations involving the author's clients and friends. However, the names and other identifying characteristics have been changed to protect the privacy of those involved. Any resemblance to actual persons (living or dead) or event is purely coincidental.

Finding Authentic You Publishing
Copyright © 2016
Printed in the United States of America.
All rights reserved. No part of this book may be reproduced in any form or by any electronic or mechanical means, including information storage and retrieval systems, without permission in writing from the publisher, except by a reviewer, who may quote brief passages in a review. We here at Finding Authentic You Publishing enjoy hearing from readers.
www.FindingAuthenticYou.com
www.BoSebastian.com

10 9 8 7 6 5 4 3 2

Cover Art and Design: David Menton

Interior Design: Bo Sebastian

TABLE OF CONTENTS

7 Steps to Effective Change 7

Discovery 1: Momma Lost Her Cool & Her Credit Card 20

Discovery 2: Like a Dog Returning to It's Vomit 23

Discovery 3: Change Your Mind, Change Your World 25

Discovery 4: Revelations—The Awakening Process 27

Discovery 5: Dust in the Wind 29

Discovery 6: Dealing with Frustration 31

Discovery 7: Hitting Rock Bottom, A Right of Passage 33

Discovery 8: Are You Listening 35

Discovery 9: A Long and Winding Road 38

Discovery 10: Make a Clear Decision 41

Discovery 11: She Wrote "I Love You" in Lipstick 43

Discovery 12: Exponential Resource 45

Discovery 13: Just How Connected Are We to the
    Heavenly World? Part I 47

Discovery 14: Just How Connected Are We to the
    Heavenly World? Part II 51

Discovery 15: Self-Inquiry 54

Discovery 16: Safe Boundaries 56

Discovery 17: The Bad Choices that Wake Us 59

Discovery 18: An Ally for Your Dreams 62

Discovery 19: How Does Prayer Work? 65

Discovery 20: Is Love Enough?...67

Discovery 21: Walking the Path...71

Discovery 22: Getting Older...72

Discovery 23: Our Social Networking World...........................74

Discovery 24: What? A Roach in My Kitchen!........................76

Discovery 25: When Is Enough, Enough?................................78

Discovery 26: The Murky Waters of the Mind.......................81

Discovery 27: Bored but Not Broken..83

Discovery 28: Fixing What's Not Broken................................86

Discovery 29: Reality or Fantasy...88

Discovery 30: The Element of Surprise...................................91

Discovery 31: The Answer to How is *Yes*................................94

Discovery 32: Who Am I Without Him or Her?....................98

Discovery 33: Stop, Look, Listen!..101

Discovery 34: Self-Soothing..104

Discovery 35: Belief, Passion, Desire—Action.....................107

Discovery 36: Letting Go...109

Discovery 37: The Secret to a Successful Relationship.....111

Discovery 38: Are You Really Asking for
  What You Want?...114

Discovery 39: Dragonfly..117

Discovery 40: Every Moment with You Is a Gift................120

Discovery 41: Finding Your True Purpose 123

Discovery 42: We Can Be One Two-gether............................126

Discovery 43: Raise Your Self-Worth......................................129

Discovery 44: Limitless Self-Worth with Surrender 131

Discovery 45: Not Easy, but Powerful 134

Discovery 46: How Deep Are Your Roots..............................137

Discovery 47: What Does Your Personal Warning Label Say? 139

Discovery 48: Failure Is an Ugly Word....................................142

Discovery 49: Our Deepest Desire Is... 144

Discovery 50: Gateway to Happiness.....................................146

Epilogue 149

About the Author: 151

Finding Authentic You

(This book was published well before I began to extend my belief far past my Christian upbringing. Much of this book is spoken with and reflects the ideas of a man who had his beginning in Christianity. This is not meant to distract anyone from his or her current belief. As a former Christian minister, I often reflect on stories from the Christian and Judaic beliefs to show examples of how those truths became ways to steer me into new directions and develop a deeper and wider understanding of God and of life.)

Seven Steps to Effective Change

I sometimes search outward for things that qualify me as a person. But, I always go inward for that which quantifies me for greatness.

As human beings, we are ever evolving from the time we are conceived until the time our spirit leaves the body in death. Sometimes there is growth and sometimes decline. But one thing is absolutely certain, change always happens.

We are spirits dwelling in physical, human flesh. Most of us consider that spirit is unchangeable by definition. So, by being human, your spirit is forced to enter on a pathway of time where change is not only necessary—but also inevitable.

The creation of something new from the change or metamorphosis of something already existing is as old as time. When leaves from deciduous trees fall to the ground, they make mulch and fertilize the ground for the next year. Coal is pressurized over thousands of years to make diamonds. The irritant, a grain of sand in an oyster, changes to a beautiful pearl. Existing water from floods and swamps evaporate to form clouds, which eventually produce rain, which make crops grow, then feed the world. So, also from the sometimes-battered wreckage of our pasts, something new and wonderful is being created right now in the world, in you... in me.

Step One:
Recognize That Change Is Inevitable

Have you ever heard the saying, "I'm like a picture, developing from the negative"? The truth of this statement in your life is the genesis of our journey together toward effective and necessary change.

I don't believe joy can be experienced while a person is resistant to change. Change is always present and always knocking on our door, every moment, every second of every day.

> *Not one moment in time exists without the next moment in time forcing it to become history.*

Change, therefore is inevitable. It is an integral part of every human being's life.

Sometimes when I receive a phone call from one of my crazy friends, and I know by the *Caller ID* who it is, I'll answer the phone: "This is the Betty Ford Center for Inevitable Change! May I help you become less of what you want to be and more of what I want you to be?"

If you are one of my close friends, you would probably expect that I would lead with something pithy or smart ass. The truth, though, I truly feel that my life... our lives... are here on this earth for an evolution of sorts, which definitely involves change.

You can be one of those people who:

1. gets coerced into change by harsh life experiences,

2. one of those people who has drama all around pushing you to change,

3. experiences a traumatic event that forces you to change, or

4. you can be open to change daily, and ultimately be happy about it.

Personally, I prefer the latter. I don't like to fight. I never have. I'm certainly not about fighting an unproductive battle against reality. Which one of us can plan what truly happens today and know with certainty our plans will happen exactly as we intended?

I can think of many things that look negative on the surface, but hiding beneath the surface is something new and wonderful. I remember one specific instance, an impending operation on my foot. It was a simple procedure, but there was pain involved to get to the place where I would be feeling better. I didn't want the pain. In fact, after having had the surgery, had I known how much pain I would have been in, I may have opted not to have the optional surgery.

However, now that I am healed of the pain, I am thankful that I went through the misery of the operation to take care of my discomfort in my foot. I'm sure you can think of hundreds of things you have done in your life that on the surface, you may not do again, but as a result, you benefitted.

Step Two:
Release from Resistance to Change

I work with all sorts of different problems as a Life & Health Coach and Clinical Hypnotist. With this one specific man, we were dealing with relationship issues. He was having trouble committing.

One balmy week in summer my client told me that his mother was in town for a visit. I gently suggested that she come in with him for his next session. He didn't think it was a problem, so we invited her.

This particular man had trouble with monogamy. So, he invites his mother into the conversation by asking her in his New York, Italian accent, "Ma, did you think that you could be monogamous to Dad when you married him?"

She appeared to be a little reserved, sitting right at the edge of the couch beside him. She fidgeted her hands. "Well— you— see— hmm... Ah, no."

Honestly, I was pleasantly shocked by her forthright answer.

The son goes on, "Well, Ma, when you married Harry, did you think you could be monogamous then?"

She looked at me, then at him. "Mhhh, no!"

"How about Carl?" my client asks, now incredulous.

His mother moved so close to the front of the couch that I thought she was going to fall off. "Well, honey, maybe."

Being the good Life Coach, I smiled at his mother without judgment, then quickly focused on my client: "So, tell me, Dick, how does that make you feel?"

Richard was just about to launch into a diatribe about finally understanding why he was never able to be faithful to any of his partners, then looked at his mother and said, "Ma, you don't understanding the definition of monogamy. Do you?"

She said, after a very long pause and a puzzled face, "Ah, no."

Step Three:
Understanding What Change Is

If you don't understand how to add and subtract, you can't expect to balance your checkbook. So, you've got to understand the tools of change, before you can expect effective results. Change becomes much easier when you awaken each day believing that the now is all perfectly orchestrated. Everything is in its right place in time, even the tragedies. *Yes, even the tragedies.*

In the fifth chapter of the Christian gospel according to Matthew, the Master Teacher, Jesus, gives us some finer understanding of the meaning of change. This is what He says in the Beatitudes, from the translation, **The Message**:

> *...You're blessed when you're at the end of your rope. With Less of you, there is more of God...*
>
> *You're blessed when you feel you've lost what is most dear to you. Only then can you be embraced by the One most dear to you...*

If this is true, then I am led to believe that Jesus was saying that all things are in divine order, and letting go of what we believe to be the end result is the key. All that you think, all that you experience, all that you are is not just an accident. And the tools of change are right within your grasp. The tools of change are everything that you are grappling with today. They are every problem at work or in your relationships. But, you just have to acknowledge them and allow spirit to further define how to deal with each problem.

With a deeper look at your personal issues, you may just discover that what you see around you is drawing you into the most effective change your soul needs at this very moment... to be happy.

Step Four:
A History Lesson—About You.

About ten years ago, I wrote my third novel, *Fatal Virtues—The Color Red*. Initially, I had trouble making the heroine palatable and affable. I created her the perfect Catholic woman—intelligent, beautiful, and she cared about her family to the point of almost destroying her own life.

I knew enough about my character's past to breathe life into her, but something remained missing. Then, the answer occurred to me. My heroine needed a personal problem, something from her past plaguing her. Right? What person doesn't have some part of her youth she wishes she could change?

So, I took this perfect, Catholic girl and made her initially become a nun. However, she was unable to keep her vows, fell in love, and later decided to become a lawyer to help her Mafia family. The viewer would now see this character as someone he or she could related to, being able to understand that virtually no one could stay honorable and dedicated to a life of celibacy, but certainly would try to help family, no matter how tragic their problems were.

Seeing her flaws actually makes you want her to be a better person. Now she becomes more of a heroine whenever she overcomes her darkness.

Why is that so? Why do we feel more comfortable with people who have flaws? Why do we like the contestants on *The Voice* who have tainted pasts and make glaring pitch mistakes, better than the ones who are perfect and on pitch? Why do we follow movie stars who have become addicts and then welcome their recovery like they are Prodigal Sons and Daughters?

And the best question... and you know you've been asking yourself this for many years: Why on God's green Earth did your high school sweetheart pick that skanky redneck to marry when he could have had... perfect you?

I'll tell you the hard answer to that question. The woman that old boyfriend married probably wasn't afraid to show her flaws. And you were. Your old sweetheart probably felt more comfortable with his new partner because of that reason.

You are the hero in Creator's story. It doesn't serve the world or anyone in your life to pretend to play your role perfectly or without flaws. We all know you have flaws. In fact, having problems makes you real, more likable, and more able to reach through your own foibles to develop compassion in yourself and for others.

* * *

I was the leader of a rather large spiritual community in Nashville, and a great deal of people counted on me for support. But one year, I had broken up from an eight-year relationship—whom I thought was the love of my life. He left me devastated. I couldn't stop crying... In those times I learned this important lesson:

> *That my sorrow and my brokenness made me easier to love and to care for.*

I had many friends later share with me how, though they remained saddened to see me distressed, they also saw how open to those around me comforting me I had become. In those moments, I also saw who my trusted friends were. I can see now that the most compassionate thing in that moment of my life was to let others take care of me, as I had taken care of them in the past.

The Fifth Step:
Look at Your Past with Compassion

Researching your past is much like writing my novel and doing the research to create a palatable character. What you are now is made of all the parts you were in the past. So, you must ask yourself questions like:

1. What are your social, political, and religious views?
2. Did you development them yourself, or were they imposed upon you?
3. Was there some trauma in your past that has changed the way you view the rest of your life?
4. And my favorite question: What part of your human anatomy fondly resembles your aging relatives?

To make effective change you must discover what part of your thinking is actually yours and what was simply fed to you or *done* to you. In doing so, you have to sift out what no longer serves your life and replace those ways of thinking with ways that do serve you.

Life is like a threshing floor.

Read the following statement aloud: "I release and let

go of all things that no longer serve my life. I am open and willing for change!"

After doing so, check out your body. Were you barely moving your lips? Were your legs crossed, arms crossed, or your lips so tight they are turning white? Admit it! Everything you have ever let go of in life had claw marks in it.

Change takes openness. And commitment. And true authenticity about everything that has happened to you in your past.

The Sixth Step:
Making a Strong Commitment to Change

Let's try repeating this bold statement again. Aloud. This time with meaning. With your palms and arms open:

> *I release and let go of all things that no longer serve my life. I am open and willing for change.*

Let's look at some of the questions you can ask yourself concerning your past history:

- How did your family life affect you? This is a huge question. But, to undo unproductive thinking, you often have to rediscover your family life patterns, and see how you're reliving them NOW. No one likes to hear you are acting like your mother or father. But the truth is, sometimes we do. I know I can be a very controlling, just as my dad was, if I don't watch myself with an authentic and compassionate eye.

- What traits are you holding of your parents that you want to let go of today?

- To make it easier, let's focus on just one trait and make a commitment for change in just this one area.

Everyday I hear stories from clients that change me, make me look deeper into my own soul for understanding. When I find myself drifting off into my own head and thoughts, while a client is sharing his or her story, I force myself back into the present moment and listen harder. I do this because I know that what my client shares is probably something I am avoiding in my own self.

We are all like mirrors to each other. When I look at you or am bothered by you, you hold up a mirror to a part of me that I don't want to address. I need to look at this part of myself to become a better person.

If you don't question your thoughts, you are not growing spiritually. This practice of self-exploration didn't happen overnight for me. In fact, it has taken me many years to realize that all that I have in this world is right here in this moment. I can choose to waste the moment, keep reliving it over and over with the same unproductive thoughts and unproductive actions, or be open and free to experience the next moment of precious life.

The Seventh Step:
Dream Your Awesome Future

As I write this book, I am creating a vision board of what I want this book to be, who I want it to touch, and where I would like to travel with it. What is in my mind, will produce in kind in my life.

I believe in the principles of spirit-born enthusiasm. The etymology of the word *enthusiasm* has two Greek root word: **En** – which mean within, and **Theos** – which means God.

Finding Authentic You

Spirit constantly can direct us to a path that is within God's perfect will for each of us. You don't have to be afraid that Spirit's desire for you will be something you don't desire for yourself. You have been created specifically for what you are to accomplish in this world. Go forth and become your greatest self!

One Year of Effective Change:

The rest of this book will fill in the blanks for you and expound upon each step with simple, yet bold, ideas about finding your Authentic Self. I will walk through these steps with you and show you how each step affects the body and the inner workings of the mind.

Along the way, I will share poignant and inspiring stories of change from my professional career as a Life Coach and a Consulting Clinical Hypnotist that will drive you toward your greatest evolution.

We will do this interactively and in groups. You can create your own group; look for groups in your close proximity, and also correspond with me through the website FindingAuthenticYou.com. I will also provide a weekly challenge to correspond with your work in this book via a my website: www.BoSebastian.com. Click on the Year to CLEAR button.

Accept that the best you can be is ready for you right now!

Finding Authentic You

THE DISCOVERIES

Discovery 1: Momma Lost Her Credit Card and Her Cool!

My mom and I went grocery shopping at the local grocery story. When it came time to pay for her groceries, she started freaking out. I looked behind me to find a frazzled woman throwing things out of her pocketbook and hollering crazy sounds like a mad woman: "I can't find it. Where did I put it? I know it's here. It has to be here? How stupid I am. Where can it be?"

"What's going on?" I asked her, trying to calm her.

"I lost my bank card. How will I pay for the groceries? Oh my God, what if someone stole it, and they used all my money!"

These were all valid reasons to be frightened in a world where identity theft for an elderly person is not only quite probable, but very likely. I took her hand and asked her to let me help her look. We scoured the purse. I never knew there could be so many compartments with things wrapped in tissues in one purse—things I was afraid to unfurl.

Then, I discovered something—about 25 of my business cards. She had been collecting them from when I first started making my first design, ten years ago. It was as if I had walked through a time warp, sifting through them, looking for her bank card.

A sweet moment turned into a sad one, when I realized that her card was, indeed, nowhere in her purse or wallet. "I'll pay for the groceries, Mom, and we'll take care of checking other places when we get you home."

She breathed heavily. When your 80-year-old mother suffered a triple by-pass a year before, you start to worry about the times that make her weary and disoriented. I took her by the arm and led her to the car, trying to ease her mind. "I'm sure we'll find it."

When we got home, we looked in all the places it could

have been, and still no card. My mother had become desperate. She was calling herself stupid, now, which in my house is not something you do. Enough name calling for an entire lifetime happened in my youth. We are all humans who make human mistakes.

I told her about the three times I left my credit card at a bar because the bartender had taken to starting a tab for me. As I wasn't used to that, I just left the bar without it. (I purposely left out the part that I was a little too tipsy to remember the credit card.) But it was easily recovered, once I remember what I did with it.

I asked her where the last place she had used the bankcard. It turned out she had used it at Walmart. She couldn't get it to work in the machine and asked the cashier to help her. She must have forgotten to get the card back from him. So, we called Walmart. Low and behold, the card was there, and everything got back to homeostasis.

I learned a lot about my mother and about myself on that day. I saw a time go by when my father or *her* stepfather would have degraded her and called her names for being so irresponsible. After her father died when she was three, she had it hard growing up with a mean, drunken, stepfather, who would often send the three siblings to bed without food, and then fall asleep on the kitchen table drunk with his face in the center of a Boston cream pie.

She married my father, who was a narcissist and wanted everything to be perfect. He wanted to portray to everyone else that he was the flawless man. He would give everyone else his time and money to live up to his narcissistic fantasy of himself, but leave the family in need, both mentally and physically.

In that moment when I was helping my mother, I realized I wasn't just helping her, but I was helping myself heal from the past. A lot of people wonder how a 50-year-old man could take care of his aging mother without going crazy. To tell you the truth, without this time to have healed all the wounds we made together, I don't think I would be the stronger, peaceful man I am today. A lot of my healing, even in the relationship arena, had to do with my relationship to my mom.

> *Sometimes life gives us the opportunity to go back into our past and amend our hearts and minds, which is so important to our mental equilibrium.*

After my mother left my father and I spent the next eight years without a mother as a young boy, I now know that I needed those years *with my mother* that were stolen from me. It doesn't matter that I'm getting the years back as an adult. What matters is that God has had the grace, and I have had the sense to see that the move to take my mother into my home was for my own good as well as my mother's.

Discovery 2: Like a Dog Returning to It's Vomit

We all go back to our old habits once in a while, even though we know that the habit will probably prove to us—once again—that we had made the correct decision the first time we left our habit. You have got to wonder about human instinct and our desire to make wrong decisions over and over again. Isn't this the definition of insanity?

Many people come to me as a clinical hypnotist, because they can't stop thinking of a lover or partner who is no longer in his/her life. I ask that person what the reason may be for the insistent desire. Usually, the answer is something such as, I originally left because he hit me, or she couldn't keep her pants up, or he was emotionally unavailable. But yet, this person can't seem to stop loving the avoidant lover, abuser, and adulterer. We literally have to do a mass brain clean-up to get to the part of the mind that will change the neural pathway to something positive, whenever a thought of the old lover comes to mind.

A hypnotist really can't stop anyone from remembering another person or action. But a good hypnotist can keep you remembering the reason why that person isn't in your life anymore. The problem with the human mind is that we only want to remember good times. The bad times we like to erase rather quickly.

Would a mother honestly want to give birth more than once if she actually remembered the entirety of the pain of childbirth? Maybe not. Could we get through life if we remembered all of the horrendous things in our lives as if they just happened?

I don't think I could. I think humanity is hardwired to forget bad and remember good. This is a great human attribute for all of us. I know that for me, having suffered an abusive childhood, I don't want to go around carrying that burden with me everywhere I go. I just as soon forget it all.

Here is a trick I learned in hypnosis. It's an NLP (Neurolinguistic Programming) trick. Give yourself a physical trigger, such as touching your face or pinching your hand, to remember the negative action that happened, so that you don't go back like a dog to its vomit.

Pinch your finger really hard and say to yourself at the same time, "_____ really broke my heart. She cheated on me with my brother. He/she doesn't deserve to ever have my love again!" Then pinch your finger again and say it over. Do this three times. Make sure that the pinch is locked in your brain with the words.

The words could be: "Smoking has been killing me for years. It has stolen my money and robbed me of years of life. Smoking makes me stink and keeps me from people I love." You could say: "Drugs have been killing me for years. They have stolen my money and robbed me of life. They cause me to make foolish decisions and keep me from people I love."

You might consider: "Working with _____ was a bad, bad experience. She showed up late. She never did her share of the work. She was a bad influence on me. I will never work with her again."

These are just a few examples of trigger statements you can say while doing something like pinching a finger, poking your fingernail into your thumb, or pinching your ear. Make the action hurt just enough to remember it with the statement. Then the next time you think about that person or job, you'll have a trigger in your subconscious that overrides your forgetfulness about how someone hurt you or did you wrong.

Discovery 3: Change Your Mind: Change Your World

Editing your thoughts sounds like something only a book editor of twenty years would come up with. But, trust me, many sages suggest to "take every thought into cavity." Your thoughts deeply effect what transpires in your daily life.

I come from a family of six children. My brother and I are as diverse as an apple is from an orange. We were brought up by the same parents, shared the same room, and even went to some of the same schools. Yet, he turned to drugs and alcohol very early in life and was in jail for the first time at eighteen. I often wonder, what made the difference in us?

I believe it was our thought process. I had a winning belief system because of an older married couple who lived next door. My brother had a gaggle of bad boys consistently goading him to try more and more detrimental behavior.

Mary and Emil took me in as if I were their son. They couldn't have children of their own, but they loved me like I was theirs. As I write this, tears fill my eyes just thinking about the amount of love that came from Mary, especially. She would wait by her side door, which was right across from our front door, until I came home from school. I'd see her peek out from the door, so none of the other children would notice.

Her small, chubby finger would curl up to indicate that she wanted me to come and visit. I'd throw down my book bag and run over to her house almost every day, especially after the fourth grade, when my mother left my father, eagerly waiting for some amazing treat she would have made.

Mary was my salvation. She taught me to believe in myself. She helped me understand that what went on in my home was an anomaly, and that I was special, despite how I was treated. I kept up the school studies and made straight A's, because I knew I wanted out from under the pain that had befallen me.

Mark, my brother, on the other hand, didn't have any savior. He was an altar boy, and even God, he rejected, when the priests mistreated him. He would steal the wine right from the church and get drunk on it. I guess, anyone could see what kind of life he would attract from that kind of thinking.

You see that my life is a constant reminder to me that a strong, positive mind attracts a strong, positive life. Everything I have ever set out to do in my life, I have accomplished. I have not succeeded in any huge way in most things, but I have experienced them, nonetheless, just by believing I could.

Someone long ago told me how to create a vision book. Get a scrapbook. In the book, place pictures and words from magazines that you have cut out that represent dreams you desire. So, one night I stopped at *Michael's Art Supply,* bought a scrapbook, and some tape. After I got home, I began looking through magazines and cut out pictures of novels and books, places I wanted to travel, stages I wanted to be on, movies I wanted to be in, kitchens I wanted to cook in, people I wanted to help. You name it, I put it in that scrapbook.

After I created the book, I put it on my bookshelf and didn't much think about it after that. When I moved from that particular home, several years later, I found the scrapbook, a bit tattered and torn. I thumbed through the pages. To my amazement, I had completed almost everything in the book. I even was driving the car I never expected to have the money to buy.

Unlimited thinking brings a world of unlimited possibility.

Discovery 4: Revelations—The Awakening Process

Lots of theologians believe that we are in the midst of what the Christian bible calls "Revelations," referring to the last book of the New Testament. This book defines the end times of our human existence, as we know it now, and gives us signs to know what to expect when these times are upon us.

When a perfect storm devastates major parts of our country, the Middle East war continues and Israel's function in it is central, and there is a rise in drugs and gang related deaths, and ISIS has made a strong statement with bombs all over the world. You would have to wonder if we aren't in some kind of awakening process, if not a time when some strong negative presence is looming over the world.

Everything that goes on around us, including world power struggles such as 9-11, draw all of us in to one single consciousness. We define ourselves differently because of these acts of terror.

As I watched the television during the 9-11 crisis, I remember feeling the sentiment and compassion of the world focusing its love and care on all the people in harm's way. How important is it that we recognize this tremendous world power we have a social conscious?

Together, as a positive whole, we can change the course of history, just as our prayers change the direction of someone suffering from disease and pain. Our compassionate thoughts cumulatively pave pathways of safety for those we love!

You tell me. Why are you praying, if you don't believe prayer has power? Why are you reaching out, if you don't believe your thoughts and compassion can somehow relieve some of the pain that is going on around you? Or if you do believe your prayers are effective, then, how far can your belief take you on the road toward understanding? Can you believe in a miracle in the midst of the chaos?

"Where two or more are gathered, there I AM in their midst." This is a quote from the Master Jesus, who suggested that if one person prays, that's wonderful. But when more than one prays for the same thing, their prayers exponentially multiply.

What does a prayer do, actually?

By my definition, prayer opens up spiritual communication with a higher source. If we all tap into that higher source (no matter what we choose to call that power), can the will of that higher source be changed?

If you follow quantum physics, you know that all time is happening at once—which is hard to conceive in a 3-dimensional world. But it would explain a great deal of the strange dreams I have.

We pray with faith, hoping that there is a God who listens and takes care of our loved ones. Without this hope, most of us would feel very fearful.

So, cling to your belief now, more than ever. We are in a time where the atmosphere of change is happening many times quicker than it has ever changed in history. Something huge is on the horizon. Wouldn't you like to be spiritually ready for it?

Take the time to pray and meditate every day. Later in the book I'll share some ways I accomplish this.

Discovery 5: Dust in the Wind

One of the sayings that changed my life forever is from a book called *What Happy People Know*, by Dr. Dan Baker. He quotes one of his dying patients who had struggling through a bout of cancer only to find another small growth: She says about the meaning of life: *"Every moment that's ever been, or ever will be, is gone the instant it's begun. So life is loss. And the secret of happiness is to learn to love the moment more than you mourn the loss."* Notice she doesn't say, "But the secret of happiness..." She says, "And the secret of happiness is..."

We don't know what today or tomorrow or even the next moment will bring to our lives. We don't know if it will bring something wonderful or something tragic. But the secret to happiness is to learn to love the moment that you are in, more than the loss of it, whether good or bad.

This concept completely changed my way of thinking. I don't get up in the morning thinking that I have to change the world. I get up in the morning knowing that every moment I am conscious of the present, I am changing the world because I am conscious. Can you grasp the concept? It's huge. The songwriter Kerry Livgren wrote:

> *All we are is dust in the wind. Same old song. Just a drop of water in an endless sea. All we do crumbles to the ground though we refuse to see. Dust in the wind. All we are is dust in the wind.*

We can look at this song with a fatalistic, realistic point of view and get very sad. But when we see the truth in it, we recognize that we can't stop change, growth, or death. If this is the case, then why are we living in the past 90%

of the time? Why are we not stepping forward into life 100% of the time with vitality and love and generosity and compassion? Can you answer that question in your life and be honest?

We feel comfortable with the past. We love the idea that we are temporal beings. Maybe this comfort somehow makes us less responsible for what goes on around us. After all, we're going to die anyway. Why waste time changing the world or becoming enlightened?

You see through a glass dimly. You are living in a very crucial point in time where it is necessary to break through the fog of the past and throw ourselves into the now—fully present.

When we do this, we will bring all of our positive energy to the surface and create change on this earth. We will make a marked change that will be respected throughout the passage of time. Not only will this belief coerce you to want to wake up each morning, but it will make future generations want to wake up happy, as well.

Finding Authentic You

Discovery 6: Dealing with Frustration

We all suffer the same frustrations when we have to call for help on any electronic or computer equipment. The last time I had a computer outage, it took me a total of four hours of phone time, six phone calls, five of which were recapitulating the same problem—going over the same several beginning steps—then finally to the advanced helpdesk that gave me the direction I needed to get my computer back and running.

Who has four hours these days to be on the phone with tech support? Meanwhile, you're trying to do all your computer work on a six-inch mobile phone that is not meant to do word processing and fulfill the needs of a computer.

What did Bo do yesterday for four hours while on hold? Choose from the points below:

1. You haven't seen the right side of my head lately in photos. Half the hair is gone from pulling it out, one hair at a time.

2. I haven't had to get a mani/pedi lately, so I gnawed off all my nails, even the toenails.

3. I haven't been out lately because I broke out in hives from the anxiety.

4. I read a book that I haven't had time to read in a long time, while I waited.

5. I took deep breaths and did yoga positions at the computer while I put the phone on speakerphone.

6. I did a combination of 4 and 5 and continued on with my day as if this is just one more thing life brings me to understand humanity.

The answer is six, of course. Why should I, or you, let

anything such as a computer take away your life source just because it's broken? Yes, the computer holds the key to many of your business prospects and endeavors, but you can't change what is. You can only deal with what is. In the present, in the moment, and with the care and compassion of a parent treating a child's precious, hurting needs.

We are not here on this Earth to play Russian roulette with ourselves every time something goes wrong in our lives. How many times a day do you let your heart race because you didn't make enough time to do all the chores on your list, because you're late to pick up a child, or caught in traffic?

Now, your heart beats so hard your blood pressure becomes way too high. You're losing precious life. You may have a heart attack if you keep this up. When the truth is, no amount of worrying can change what is.

You either need to learn to give more time for certain chores, take into account for busy traffic times, or get used to the stress that life can hand you.

Put on some nice music, a book on tape that you've been wanting to read, call the person who is waiting for you, and relax into the situation that you can't change.

Discovery 7: Hitting Rock Bottom: A Right of Passage

We've all heard the story of the alcoholic or drug addict found face down in a mud puddle after losing his friends, job, and family. Generally, this is a right of passage, as there is nowhere else to go but up, if the alcoholic faces the addiction.

I have heard many stories of hitting rock bottom, which means that an unhealthy ego has been in complete control for a long while. The person involved usually has a dark night of the soul, which can be defined as the weakest moment of your life. This is when you finally realize that accepting your spiritual truth, whatever that may be, is the only way out of despair.

My dark night of the soul was a year after I moved to Nashville. I had been an "in the closet" homosexual for many years, as I left my sexuality for the church and religion. I thought I couldn't be gay and love God at the same time. As I struggled for many years, even giving up the idea of having an intimate partner completely, I prayed for answers.

A friend recommended I go to see a counselor, who happened to be a priest at Catholic Services. My first appointment lasted for three hours. I could not stop crying. Every story I told about my past led to more tears and shame. Until that moment in my life, I felt as if my childhood had been normal. But suddenly, I realized that all of the abuse I had suffered left me with posttraumatic stress and enough anxiety to fill the Titanic.

The priest counseling me was kind and caring. He helped me through much of what could have been a nervous breakdown. He advised me that my childhood was not my fault. He showed me ways of forgiving and moving on that I had not thought of in the past.

Still, one night soon after I started therapy, I wanted to

take my life. I felt hopeless and fearful. I was too broken to ever find happiness.

I did not make any specific plans as to how I would proceed with suicide, but I thought hard about not continuing my life. I shared with my mother how sad I had been. She lived in Tucson, Arizona, then, and I lived in Nashville.

I went to get groceries later that evening. When I returned to my house, three policemen with flashlights were looking in my windows. Of course, this scared me. I thought I had been robbed, or that they had been looking for some criminal who ended up hiding in my basement.

Though it sounds funny now when I think of the scenario: my mother was so frightened that I would have actually taken my life that she called the police and told them of her fear. The words of the big, hunky policeman were what actually set me back on course, "Son, I think you better call your mom. She thought you took your life."

When I heard his words, I woke up. I had been on a spiralling tunnel going down to the darkest part of my soul. I had revisited the ugliest parts of my past only to find no doors leading to salvation. However, a door existed for me to find health and peace once again. I simply needed professional help to face my demons.

If you or someone you know has been on a dark path for some time, realize that reaching out for help may be your only choice. Trusting someone to help you is a brave move, probably the strongest move you will ever make.

Without having mental health and a stable mind, finding spirituality is moot. We must be in our right mind to begin on a path of spiritual growth. If you cannot dream clearly, you cannot create a better life for yourself. Everything begins with clarity of mind. From this clarity comes a divine connection to the Mind of God.

Discovery 8: Are You Listening?

I had been a vegetarian for 22 years when my stomach started to rebel against my *spiritual* decision to not eat meat. I tried every doctor, every holistic way to treat my stomach, but even the holistic doctors said, "Bo, you really need to start to eat meat."

What do you do when everything in your mind says *no* and everything in your physical body says *yes*?

The answer is: you listen to both. Your body is like a baby crying in the middle of the night. You listen to see if the baby needs to be fed or if she's just fussing. But you listen. If there is something drastically wrong, you will know by the kind of cry or by the ways the baby functions or doesn't function.

Your body speaks to you in nonverbal ways all of the time. Your shoulders and neck ache when you have looked at the computer for too long. Your lower back growls at you when you have spent the day lifting heavy things to help your friend move. You get a headache when you have too much anxiety for one person to handle.

All of these are signs that the body need the attention of your deductive brain. Your body needs you to stop what you are doing and rest. It needs for you to attend to the needs of the physical part of you. After all, the body is the house of your mind and spirit. Your human body is an important part of your existence here on earth. Without it, you would be dead and useless to your family, friends, and the world. The deductive process is what sorts out what is good and what is bad for you. It makes the hard choices.

So, I listened to my body after much struggle with mind and decided that despite my desire to not eat animals, I would pray that my mind could wrap itself around the idea of eating something that had died for my life. I became thankful for the sacrifice of the animal, and began to try small pieces of meat. I didn't cook it or buy it for a long time, because touching raw meat felt too close to the sacrifice. But, I did listen to the advice of the doctors and practitioners and ate some meat with lots of resistance and even tears, at first.

The practitioners were right. I immediately began to feel better and more vibrant. My stomach stopped feeling terrible all the time. I was very thankful, but at the same time a little confused. I had thought my choice to be a vegetarian was a spiritual one. Apparently, my body had a different lesson for me to learn—an even harder one.

I think this lesson prepared me for the biggest lesson of my life: GETTING OLDER. We think we can gracefully make our way into our elderly years, but the truth is: aches and pains and arthritis and disease sneak in to cramp our style right around the age of 40-50. It's no fun. But if you're not listening to your body, it's even less fun.

I'll give you the perfect example. My yoga practice used to be very intense. Some would call it the hardest kind of yoga practice. But one day, I just had to say to myself, "Bo, this just isn't feeling good anymore. In fact, it feels pretty crappy."

I had to completely modify the way I did my practice, so that my body started to feel good after yoga. After all, isn't that the entire premise of yoga?

A yoga practice isn't about getting into the hardest pose. It's about moving toward your most difficult position, and listening to your body, so you never harm your self. If the most difficult position for you is just standing still, then that is exactly what you should do.

Yoga means the union or yoking of the mind, body, and spirit. There is no union if your body is screaming and your mind isn't listening. Take a lesson from this yogi and former vegetarian. I wish I could have it my way and be all the things I was when I was twenty.

I simply can't. I have to be who I can be within the parameters of my physical self. I have to be authentic me. If that means giving up something to survive, I should do it.

Discovery 9: A Long and Winding Road

The prodigal son leaves to go on a journey far away from the protection of his father's money and love to find that separation from home is not all that he thought it would be. Empty handed and beaten down, he returns home.

The husband leaves his partner for the sexy secretary only to find that his new lover is needy, wants a father not a partner, and is completely codependent. The husband begs for the forgiveness of his partner to return to true love.

The child leaves school to marry his young love and gets a minimum wage job, only to find that responsibility and being a young father is much harder than he could have ever imagined. He goes back to his parents and asks for their support until he can go back to school and do what they intended for him.

These hard lessons metaphorically all lead us back home.

Paul McCartney sang:

"The Long and Winding Road

That Leads Me to Your Door

Will Never Disappear

I've Seen that Road Before

It Always Leads Me Here

Lead Me to Your Door..."

This is the metaphor of spiritual life. Once we have made mistakes and have left love, we become afraid to return to love's door. The bible couldn't make it clearer in the story of the prodigal son, that God is always waiting with open arms for you to come home into the love that never left you. Do not waste your time in self-flagellations and remorse. Return to love!

I have heard stories of leaving love behind because of being rejected from churches and pastors, because someone was gay or had caused some unpardonable sin like divorce. These sons and daughters of God were treated like castaways by the very people who should have supported them. I understand why someone in this situation would project that this was Spirit throwing him into the fires of an angry world and out of Grace.

Churches or pastors are not the voice of authority. If they were, I think we would all be a lot more injured than we are now. They may hope to represent God, but they certainly are not the Almighty, nor do they know your personal path to freedom and truth. You are the only one who knows your relationship with God.

I was fortunate. When I got kicked out of three churches, instead of hating God, I just assumed God was leading me in a different direction. This is how I ended up in New Thought. I wanted to be in a church that did not condemn me for being gay. I researched churches and found that New Thought preached of a loving, all forgiving God. I discovered the forgiving and loving face of God, even though I had been rejected by religion.

I know there is a reason for my life. I keep my mind and heart open every day for what this purpose might be. I want to keep waking every day to the sound of my alarm and thinking: what is going to happen today that will take me a little closer to understanding my purpose here on this earth. I want to hear myself say: This Is the Best Day Yet!

Don't you want that for your life?

If you do, what would help you connect with your spiritual oneness is the only thing that is of importance in this walk. Your connection. Not mine.

Everything leads to the one, eternal choice: your fear vs. Spirit's unlimited possibility.

Discovery 10: Make a Clear Decision

The tools to making a clear and authentic decision start with being able to separate all the deductive workings of your brain from the heartfelt push or rejection in your subconscious mind. Most people can't usually make the separation of the two halves of the brain; therefore, making a clear decision is quite difficult.

Most recently, I was faced with an extremely hard decision. The reasons in my head for going forward with the decision were tenfold, but my heart kept backing away from moving forward. I couldn't convince myself that I was making the right decision; therefore, I made no decision.

This is our usual course of action, until something forces us in one direction or the other. No one really wants to be forced into a decision. We would much rather feel the autonomy of finding that right choice on our own and having the strength to follow it through with vitality.

So, what did I do to help myself get to the right decision?

The first thing that I did was to call a friend who is a therapist. No better place exists to begin sorting out a mess in your head than with someone who is an expert at separating fact from fiction. If you have a mental health practitioner or life coach who knows you well, that's even better, because they can call you on your usual *stuff*.

My past behavior is to circumvent the problem, be a codependent, try to help and nurture the situation, instead of doing what's best for me. My therapist friend kept asking me the question I needed to hear, "What is the best move for you in this situation? What would make you feel at peace?" Finally, I had to answer that the best move for me was to go forward with my decision.

When we put our foot to the gas pedal, we don't know where we will land. We just know movement forward gets us out of our slump and disparaging situation. When I chose to step forward into my decision, I said to myself, this doesn't mean that Spirit may have a completely different solution for me. If that is true, let me drive directly into it.

Life is full of ups and downs. We know that. We can't face a day without knowing that we could be thrown a curve ball. But being able to make simple choices for ourselves and moving forward in them is an important part of life.

You have the power to move any mountain you choose. I believe that for you, and I believe that for me. And so it is.

Discovery 11: She Wrote "I Love You" in Lipstick on the Bathroom Mirror

I had a client who has been struggling with weight issues. For five weeks he has been coming to me riddled with stress from a job that had begun a vast change after 25 years of homeostasis. Today, he had an epiphany! He realized after he had read some of the material I had sent home with him (5 weeks ago...) that he had been eating emotionally.

When he would come home from work, he would feel exhausted, didn't want to exercise, and ate to fill the emptiness he felt emotionally from a detached relationship with his wife.

But, after our last session, things began to change. He learned to be a compassionate observer of his life. What does that mean?

- We can wake up in the morning and think we are our physical body, entrenched with a to-do list a mile long, which sends us into our cognitive, deductive brain. If we stay on this course throughout the day, we become robots that train our minds to listen to the habits of our body and our old thinking, instead of waiting for spiritual insight.

- Becoming a compassionate observer of our lives takes detaching from your old behavior (compulsive, fearful, anxious thinking) and beginning to look at life as if you are objectively watching someone else whom you can help. That person is YOU! We have many old neural pathways (connection in our brains linked to past knowledge and circumstance) trying to convince us we ARE our past. Only by becoming a conscious observer can we make change to these behaviors.

My client began to witness his shortcomings and

decided he wanted to make a change. As he committed to altering his emotional life, his wife saw the light as well. She had been encouraging him to get healthier, but he didn't do much about making a plan for change. She could see that and got disinterested in his lax ways about his life, including their sex life. In other words, she became disappointed and detached.

So, this morning she wrote on the bathroom mirror in lipstick: I LOVE YOU! That's all it took for my client to see that his change in awareness and behavior was making a difference, not just for himself, but for everyone he faced daily.

I suggested that writing those words was incredibly courageous and compassionate for his wife. She took that honest, loving step forward in their relationship. I told him to surprise her with some beautiful flowers and tell her he loved her, too.

I have a feeling someone is going to be rolling around in intimacy tonight and enjoying the good that becoming aware brings to our lives.

Discovery 12: Exponential Resource

I think the question on everyone's mind almost everyday is: do I have enough?

- Do I have enough money?
- Do I have enough beauty?
- Do I have enough resources?
- Do I have enough intelligence?
- Do I have enough love?

The list can go on for eternity. We all understand that need is part of the human condition. The moment we breathe air, we cry for food, for breast milk, for warmth, for comfort. Caretakers provided for us, as a general rule, most of our childhood. Then, we must begin to fend for ourselves. It is at this juncture in life, we begin to experience the sense that there MAY just not be enough of what we need to get by.

On a physical plane, there may not be enough. Plenty of people starve and go without food and clothing in this world. How do we change the instinct in our brains to grasp for everything we can get and then live beyond our means? How do we release from this fear of lack, even though we may actually have more than enough?

I had an interesting meditation a couple of days ago. I dwelled on finance. I remembered a day when I struggled to find money for rent and food. I learned the lesson of being a good businessman from a lot of talented people around me. So, for a long time, I haven't had to feel the sense of living from month to month.

Buy a home and car, let your mom move in with you, plant five gardens, remodel, and keep the business going, and you'll see that sometimes you just have to do without a vacation once a year. I have been okay with this business model.

In my prayers and meditations and affirmations, as I have done for a long time, I focus on prosperity. I imagine angels going forward and gathering clients to come to me. I see them lining up at my door. I see cars in my driveway. I see books that I've written on many bookshelves and downloaded on Kindles. I imagine interviews with Dr. Phil and Ellen. I have been very meticulous about envisioning what I want in my life for many years.

But during this particular meditation, I felt a hand on my shoulder and a voice say, "Stop! What you need to do is quit limiting what I can do for you by putting dollar signs and parameters around everything you pray for. I am a Source of unlimited means. If you let go of your quest for certainty and simply pray that I fulfill your needs, I will create exponentially more than you can ever imagine!"

I began to meditate on that prophetic word. How many times have I said to myself, "My bills are $_____ and I need ___ amount of clients this month to fulfill that need, God"?

I have been asking for a lot less than God wants to give me. If I would have just prayed, "God, you know my needs, please draw to me whatever it is that you desire to give your child. I know abundance will then follow," perhaps that would have let the hand of God to lead me to greener pastures.

All of this week I have been praying without limits. I have noticed about 10-15 times a day that I put limits on what God can do in my life. Let's commit together to quit limiting Spirit God in our lives!

Discovery 13: Just How Connected Are We to the Heavenly World—Part I

I watched an episode of ***Long Island Medium***. The show is about a woman who meets people on the street and tells them about their lives in exact detail. In so doing, she helps them make peace with people who have passed away. I was moved to tears more than once.

I watched with Sharon, who doesn't come from folks who believe in such things. So, for her to watch with me was really something. The psychic woman appeared genuine, so spot-on target with her information and seemed to be bringing spiritual guidance to people who really were searching.

I have believed in psychic energy for a long time, because I believe in the prophets and the healings of Jesus and others. Psychic energy, no matter how you try to disguise it in Christian language, is basically channeling spirit. Prophets are also channeling God, which has been taboo for years in modern Christian circles.

But as I see it, many avowed Christians are stepping beyond their constrictive beliefs, because there is definitely some validity to some of the psychic energy healers and those channeling God today. Some even purport to be channeling the spirit of Jesus. "You will judge them by their fruit."

How does it fit into our spiritual paradigm today, if we seek the light and want to move forward toward an authentic spiritual life in God?

We definitely should make room for this kind of spiritual thought in our world today. But I have a caveat. I believe that mediums are not here for personal gain or to see into the future to make your decisions for you. I believe that they are here to help us make peace with the past and, perhaps, stop us from making a terrible decision in the future. This kind of intervention happens only if our decision would throw our lives completely off course from our spiritual growth.

Let's talk about how to look for a medium who is authentic and real. First of all, never go to someone you find in the phonebook or on the back of a newspaper without a personal recommendation from someone who has experienced the medium and trusts his or her intentions. That might mean doing some digging and research, but you can afford to take the time to get the right advice. Getting the wrong medium would be like going to the wrong doctor, one with little credentials or a dirty office. Plenty of people out there dabble in the spiritual world who know little to nothing about protecting themselves from negative entities and misinformation. We don't want that for you.

Also, if the medium is authentic, he or she will not try to bilk you out of money. You will pay one fee for the session, set beforehand. Most likely, you won't be asked or invited to come back, because that should be up to you.

What about Past Life Regressions? Are they valid? I have had five. Each one led me to an interpersonal change that I would have never expected had I not gone through the experience.

What should you expect from a regression? First of all, past life regressions use hypnosis to regress you beyond this life to other lives. Of course, you would have to be of the belief system that trusts our Spirit doesn't die at our human death or just has one chance at doing things correctly here on earth.

If you are interested in Past Life Regression, you have to be a very willing participant and highly suggestible to hypnosis. If you are not, the regression can turn out to be a probing into the cognitive mind, which is not such a good idea.

Finding Authentic You

I'll give you an example of one of my regressions. From the time I was a small child in a very Caucasian town, I had been completely unprejudiced, even though most of my relatives, parents, and grandparents were prejudiced. At seven, I invited the only black girl in my grade school to my birthday party. Only two other friends showed up, because of the invite. During one of my past-life regressions, I was a young slave. I watched my father get hung and murdered by the KKK. Then I, too, was lynched and murdered.

In the regression, as I listened back to the recording, it was as if I could hear the sounds of the woods, the crackle of the fire, and the rush of the hate. I knew I had experienced this somewhere in my memory, because of how compassionate I had been to those prejudiced against even at such a young age. The vision I had during the regression was as clear to me as my life is now.

I learned a few other things about my life in that regression. I discovered who—in this existence—were my father and my mother in those lifetimes. Sometimes, relationships carry over into other lives.

Debts and love and sacrifice continue on with the same characters playing different roles, each spirit in body having to learn a different lesson in this life. Also, sexes change, which also can result in a human becoming gay, if that person takes a lot of their sexual energy into the next lifetime and comes back a different sex.

Now, I'm not telling you all this to make you think that you must, also, believe as I. I'm sharing this, because I think it is necessary to be honest all of the time. Authenticity is honesty. I've never gotten anywhere in any relationship without being completely authentic.

I plan to do that in this book with you, my readers. Take what you can from it and throw the rest away. Who knows, maybe someday, you'll find that you are faced with the idea that you may have *deja vu*. If so, you might consider thinking outside the box of your present paradigm and seek out psychic help or a past life regression.

Consider this: Once—yes, in this lifetime—I was a bible-thumping, Pentecostal preacher standing on a NYC street corner passing out "you're going to hell for being gay" tracts.

That was thirty years ago. We all change and grow. Fortunately, for me, God spoke clearly and directly, "I'm not in the box you choose to put me in. I am ALL IN ALL!"

Discovery 14: Just How Connected Are We to the Heavenly World—Part II

When I was in my early thirties, my godmother slowly perished of lung cancer. She had never smoked a cigarette in her entire life. Her husband, Uncle Johnny, had smoked about three packs a day. He had died about twenty years prior to her.

When my aunt and uncle were young, and no one knew he or she was dying of cancer from cigarettes, Elvie and Johnny would sit in a 6' x 6' den and watch television with Johnny chain smoking. Honestly, you couldn't see either of them if you walked into the den, the smoke was so thick.

As you can imagine, Aunt Elvie had become very angry at Johnny for helping her to die from a substance she never intended to use. Elvie was a tough woman. Every one of her nine brothers and sisters feared her anger. She said what was on her mind and didn't care what anyone else thought.

When it came time for her dying, no one would speak of death to her. They tiptoed around the subject. In those days, families could choose not to share with their parents about an impending death. When I finally got to the hospital from Nashville to visit, Aunt Elvie was about to die. Still, no one told her she had only a day or two to live. I was given strict instructions not to mention death.

The moment I got alone with Aunt Elvie, I asked her if she was afraid. I wanted to know if there was anything I could do for her. I wanted to see if she needed prayer. But mostly, I wanted her to know that I believed that she wasn't going anywhere but outside her body when she died. If she wanted to, I told her, she could talk to me when she passed over. I promised I would listen for her voice.

For the first time in weeks, a smile spread across her

face. She understood. I could see that her questions had been answered. She was no longer afraid of what was before her. She died that night.

A radiant light appeared at my bedroom doorway that evening, beckoning to come in. Elvie appeared as a younger lady. She sat on my bed and talked to me as if I were talking to a dear friend. She said, "I want to help people quit smoking. Can you help me do that?" I had already been trained as a hypnotherapist, but I used my practice only for vocal students then. But I was open to doing what God wanted.

"Yes, of course," I told my aunt.

She said, "All you have to do is call my name, and I will be there with you and help from this side. I'll even help guide people to your door."

From the moment I began my practice in hypnotherapy, especially with cigarette smokers, Godmother Elvie has been my guardian angel, helping from heaven. I feel her presence, still. I know that she remains the reason I have a 95% success rate.

Other friends have needed help to cross over. Those precious spirits have also aided me in my work and have come back to visit on occasion. My friend Linda comes more often than anyone else. Before she died, she gave me a silver bell for Christmas. After she died, it ended up on my bedstand without me putting it there. When she visited the first time, she told me that all I had to do was ring the bell and she would hear it and come.

We have conversations still as if she were in her human body. I don't believe spirits die. I think they live on and grow and gain intelligence and wisdom. If we let them, they will assist us as angels do. We just have to be open to it and protect ourselves from any negative influences spiritually, as well.

A simple prayer will do: "God, protect me from hearing or communicating with any spirits that are not here for my good, are not of the light, and are not sending a message that will further my spiritual growth."

We are walking side by side with angels day and night. If you don't believe me, just remember how many times in your life you have been saved at the brink of disaster.

Discovery 15: Self-Inquiry

The sun shines brightly. The birds tweet with joy. Life appears peaceful. Love presents itself all around me in great friendships and with family members. Yet, I feel something looming in the air that I'm experiencing as a threat.

Have you ever felt this before? The day is completely normal, but you feel an undercurrent of negativity?

When these times come up in my life, I do one of two things:

1. I check my body for any strange feelings or pains. If I find that there is something painful or slightly abnormal going on physically, I do a *Gestalt* exercise.

The exercise consists of meditation and imagination. See your pain sitting across from you on a chair fictionalized or individualized as a real person or part of you. Ask the feeling why it has visited you today. Then wait for an answer. Of course, you have to be willing to use your imagination, or your subconscious, to access the necessary information. You must actively listen. This could cause a conversation with two individual parts of your brain. Don't freak out! You don't have multi-personalities. You might learn in the case of your bad feeling, that a pain in your neck is suggesting that you take a day off to rest.

2. My second form of therapy is using the observing part of my mind to check in and watch my human behavior without judging it. Begin by meditating. Get comfortable. Take some long deep breaths with the inhales and exhales the same length. Move your eyeballs from left to right. Begin to relax each part of your body. Most importantly, let your imagination take over. Use the idea that angels bring wisdom and

understanding from a very peaceful God source. When you come out of meditation, you should get a sense of what you need to do to make change or why you feel sadness or grief.

Life will always be a process of balancing humanity with spirituality. If you're not comfortable with those terms, balancing your deductive brain with your inductive, dreaming thoughts. These thought processes are two very completely different ways of Self Inquiry.

Discovery 16: Safe Boundaries

When is it okay to share with someone that you are uncomfortable with how he or she is treating you or acting? I had a client who I championed today for sharing with his mother that she didn't listen to him when he talked. But when another client came in who shared he was uncomfortable with the undercurrent of sexual advances with his coworker, that same coworker did not take his words lightly. She threatened to take his life. Two very similar scenarios worked out with very different outcomes.

We don't know the circumstances of anyone's life, mind, or formative years. We don't know what kind of input parents gave that individual, if any. We don't know if he or she had been abused or threatened on the way to adulthood. We also usually don't know if someone is on a psychotropic drug that can alter his/her state of mind. All of these scenarios would lead to whether or not a person could hear a healthy message about safe boundaries from a friend, coworker, or a family member.

If someone pushes you beyond your safe boundaries, you probably are right to state your case. I would recommend starting without a conviction. I would say something very low key, giving a person a chance to justify the behavior, such as, "What you just did makes me feel a little uncomfortable. I hope you can understand that I just don't feel right doing or hearing that." Of course, say your truth in a private place, to save the recipient from undo embarrassment.

If your message goes unheard and disrespected, you may state your feelings about the situation more directly and more succinctly.

I'm the type of person who doesn't like to hurt feelings. I assume that people are always doing their best in situations. Perhaps, a person just doesn't know any

Finding Authentic You

better about something like how to treat a gay person or what not to say to him or her that would be considered offensive.

If this is the case, I may take him or her aside and say, "I know you really haven't been around a lot of gay people, but what you said just isn't cool. In fact, it is a bit offensive. I understand you didn't mean it that way. But I thought I'd share with you my feelings, so you would know for the next time that you are around a gay individual."

I would never e-mail this or text my feelings to someone out of respect and, also, to avoid misunderstanding. I believe that the spoken word and the eyes of someone stating his/her truth are very important in understanding that you mean well in your encouragement and intention to do better. How that recipient takes your comment is not your responsibility. You have done your best to convey your truth with kindness and authenticity.

You can't know exactly how anyone will respond to a request for a behavior change. Some will go ballistic. If they do, you probably don't need that person in your life. Some will get sad. This is a reasonable reaction of a compassionate person who cares about you. That person may have trouble hearing criticism because of little self-esteem. Or they simply may be having trouble adjusting to change.

Others might thank you for sharing. These are the people who I would tend to flock toward. Because you know in your heart, if someone is able to love you, even though you have an opinion that is different than his/hers, that person appreciates you with the true meaning of love.

To quote the Christian bible in 1 Corinthinians 13: 1-8:

"1 If I speak with the tongues of men and of angels, but do not have love, I have become a

noisy gong or a clanging cymbal. 2 And if I have the gift of prophecy, and know all mysteries and all knowledge; and if I have all faith, so as to remove mountains, but do not have love, I am nothing. 3 And if I give all my possessions to feed the poor, and if I deliver my body to be burned, but do not have love, it profits me nothing.

"4 Love is patient, love is kind, and it is not jealous; love does not brag and is not arrogant, 5 does not act unbecomingly; it does not seek its own, is not provoked, does not take into account a wrong suffered, 6 does not rejoice in unrighteousness, but rejoices with the truth; 7 bears all things, believes all things, hopes all things, endures all things. 8 (True) Love never fails..."

Discovery 17: The Bad Choices that Wake Us Up

I remember clearly—hunkered over myself, on the verge of passing out in a closed theater in the Broadway district in NYC—how I felt and what I prayed, "Please, God, if you get me out of here alive, I will never, ever do this again!"

It was a hot day in summer in New York City. One of my dearest friends asked me to go on a date with her to make sure this very rich and handsome man wouldn't get her drunk and try to take advantage of her. She called me her human condom. Eileen was a model and stunningly beautiful. She could have had her choice of any man. But even she had struggles with boundaries.

The guy picked us up at her apartment in a limo and popped open a bottle of Dom Pérignon on the way to a five star restaurant.

I am a lightweight. Two drinks and I'm completely drunk. I decided I would pass on the champagne, while the two dates drank. I was young and hadn't experienced much of life, especially anything that was fancy.

The limousine amazed me, and the way Mr. Hotshot threw around money to get what he wanted at the restaurant was even more intriguing. We ate at the best table, got served by the best waiter, had the best of everything. The chef even came to our table with special appetizers made just for us.

I had to go the restroom after the first course, and Eileen's man friend followed me. I went into the stall. Before I had the chance to lock it, he pushed the door open and quickly closed it behind him, leaving me within two inches of his face. I became surprised and shocked at the same time. The dude had a line of cocaine on a beautiful blue glass. He snorted half the line and handed me the plate and the little glass straw.

Without thinking, I drew in the line of white powder. He snickered. He had gotten what he wanted. He trapped me, coerced me, and intrigued me without even trying. The power of money and stature robbed my very young and innocent mind of every boundary.

When I got back to the table, he ordered more champagne. Suddenly, I didn't care about drinking or about being a human condom for Eileen. I started to indulge. Before I knew it, there were three empty bottles of Dom Pérignon on the table in front of me and no Eileen and no Mr. Hotshot.

The check had been paid. I sat alone in a restaurant on the upper West Side without a clue of how I would get home or even stand up. Cab fair wasn't in my budget, so I had to ride the train. Before I could remember what happened or how I arrived there, I was doubled over in the front of a closed Broadway theater praying: "Please, God, help me get home."

A wave of energy and peace came over me. I felt as though two angels held me on both sides until I got into my apartment safely and into bed. I never again tried drugs or have drunk more than three drinks at one sitting, let alone an entire bottle and a half of champagne.

The next morning, besides a terrible headache, all I could think of was how I had let down my dear friend. If I had barely made it home alive, what had become of her? It turned out that she had much more control than I had. It was my night to learn a lesson, not hers.

We all have these times in our lives when we sink so low that the only way out remains a Divine Intervention. I know that my faith has only grown stronger since that day.

When we see others spiraling down or moving toward a place that looks like hell, we have to take into account that their moment with Divine Destiny may be straight ahead of them. Yes, of course, it could be in death, but it

Finding Authentic You

could also be a miraculous move toward positivity. We are not in control of the world or anyone else. But a powerful hand exists in the universe directing our movements and drawing us closer to understanding ourselves. I know this power intimately, and it can level the heaviest burden.

What keeps you from believing in something greater than you? If you could move away every barrier that religion has imposed upon you, could you conceive of a creator that wanted you to be whole, complete, and happy?

If this is true, begin your quest today. Stop limiting your life to what you know with certainty. Open your heart to something that takes faith to believe. I'm sure, if you look hard enough, that "something" is right in front of you.

Discovery 18: An Ally for Your Dreams

Most times the problem with reaching any goal happens between your own ears. Your mind is the crucible that often melts a very strong plan of desire with doubt and fear. It's not enough that you get rejection letters and doors closed, but even your own self can't stand proudly with you on your best ideas. Why is this so?

When you have a dream you want to fulfill, there are many ways to set up roadblocks to stop its fruition. But are you the one causing these roadblocks?

In life coaching one of the primary focuses teaches people to achieve dreams. First, you have to create a dream that you can conceivably attain. Then you must plant seeds in your subconscious mind—seeds of belief and trust that you will get to your goal.

Let's look at the physical wiring of a human being. From the moment we are conceived, we begin developing synapses and neural pathways in the brain from behaviors that exist all around us. Are we responsible for most of them? Absolutely not.

When we were too young to make decisions for ourselves, parents and people who took care of us created most of our initial, behavior triggers in the brain. Why would Spirit set up life so that we would be plagued as adults with the programming of parents who probably had no idea how to condition a healthy mind?

In my situation, I did get a lot of motherly love before she snuck out one summer afternoon after third grade. I lacked in the fatherly love arena. I had five siblings, so getting attention was about being an overachiever. My eldest sister taught me to play the piano at six. Within a year, I began to exceed her. I had to be the best, if I wanted to gain the attention of my father.

I watched as he demeaned all the rest of the children

Finding Authentic You

for their lack of ambition and desire to study. So, I came home with straight A's every six weeks, over achieving again. But, fortunately, this set me up to be an excellent candidate to have a great career, no matter what I chose.

If you look at my brother's scenario, his was almost the opposite. My father tried to instill in him the desire to do all the things in which my father excelled. My brother rebelled. So, instead of gaining praise, he got beaten. This set my brother up to be an underachiever, even though he struggled for the same thing I did—Daddy's approval.

I can still hear my brother's voice on the phone a few years ago. I hadn't spoken to him since my father died ten years ago. He had moved three times and never gave anyone in the family his address. But being savvy and ambitious, I helped my mother find him. We called him at work one day. The first thing he said to me was, "Dad never loved me!"

He didn't say, "Hey, how are you doing?" or "What have you been doing?" or "How the hell did you get my number?" No, he just began unloading about how his father didn't give him the support he needed to survive.

He did speak to my mother. Mom tried to give him love. But the paradigm of never getting enough, early enough, makes it hard to fill the gaping hole that is left as an adult. I tell you this story, because so many of us have the same kind of drama and workings in our brains that cause our best ideas and dreams to get the kibosh when we begin to hear the voices of the past tell us that we will never succeed and that our ideas are worthless.

This moment in time manifests extreme importance, realizing that your emotional brain is an amalgam of human input, which is mostly error. So, when error thoughts come up, you have to be of sound mind enough to realize that these thoughts are not your adult, present thoughts. You have to slip into the frontal cortex of the brain and become an objective, compassionate observer of yourself and speak kind words to your own mind in the place of the old negative thoughts.

You've heard of affirmations. This is the same concept, but with more push toward understanding why you must have an arsenal of strong positive input to deflect the negative.

If you don't make this change in your mind when you hear error voices, your ideas will drown in a cesspool of negativity, I guarantee it. You will never see your dreams come true.

If you must be a fighter, battle the thoughts in your brain. Choose positive, affirmative thoughts that will eventually create prosperity, great relationship, and peace.

Discovery 19: How Does Prayer Work?

I've often wondered if Spirit actually leads to pray when someone needs prayer, or if someone needing prayer causes me to pray. If either of these scenarios makes a difference, why would a God who knows all, sees all, creates all, need my prayers to change the course of action on Earth? This remains a big question in a big world.

I take my thoughts to a quiet place and contemplate answers. From this place of peace I write. This is what I heard as I prayed:

> *"Prayer is not a begging, prayer is not an earnest asking, prayer is not a demand for God to do anything different than what is planned as the best for humanity or an individual.*
>
> *"Prayer is, in fact, a way to connect you to the whole. Prayer is a way for you to understand sickness and disaster. It is a way for you to make peace within your heart. It is not a way to change God's mind.*
>
> *"Prayer is a conversation or a meditation with the holiest part of your being—a mediation, if you will, with the best part of the best of you."*

When someone experiences healing from prayer, this is a manifestation of the power of the whole body of Christ thinking as one in harmony with Good. When someone doesn't experience healing in the same situation, the power of the whole must help a soul cross over to a heavenly existence and out of the human existence.

Jesus found his Oneness with God. He asked in His heart what God needed of Him. He expressed with nonresistance and peace what was to come through the truest power of belief. He created what was real through Spirit and made it matter. He was the ultimate prayer warrior. He taught us to pray.

Our father who dwell in a heavenly place, your name is to be honored. Someday, we all hope that the Earth will become as peaceful as the place in which You dwell.

Please inspire us with all we need to know. Forgive us when we misunderstand.

Let us resist the temptation to want more. Keep our bodies healthy and our minds in the spirit of positivity.

For this is God Eternal living through us, in us, and as us.

Discovery 20: Is Love Enough?

In my many tries at love, the one glaring question that sticks out: IS LOVE ENOUGH? You know it, I know it, the 18-year-old finding first love doesn't know it, the young Southern Belle who marries for stature knows it, the two lovers who meet on a Vegas vacation and marry don't know it....

When is love enough?

Let's define love in intimate relationships. Love is not carnal desire or passion. Love is a deep respect for another person. Love is a subconscious drive that presses you forward into unchartered emotions when you become afraid. Love is built on trust, security, and faith. But mostly love is about giving each other space to breathe, to grow, and to be the support under which the manifestations of dreams come forth.

That being said, is that enough to make relationship work? The unfortunate answer is *no*. The one important feature in relationship that people never discuss until it's too late is a couple's journey toward the same destiny. This could be as simple as "Do you want to watch the same television shows at night?" Because if you don't, there goes three hours wasted, when you are completely separated and could be enjoying something together.

A relationship not working could be as simple as "I love wearing cologne." The challenge, "I'm allergic to cologne. It gives me migraines."

Life could be as grand as, I have enough money in my bank account to go travel to Hawaii every two month to surf, and you have to stay at home and work. But I still want to go for two weeks every other month.

It could be two great people with two diverse jobs, one requiring many hours divested in intricate thinking and the other in a job that is completely peaceful. Each now has a different way of wanting to rest. Who gets to have peace and who wants to go out dancing?

Not working a regular job may be the opposite of too good. This happens when two people have almost everything in common, and they both share great entrepreneurial expertise and work at home. They simply get sick of being around each other.

The one huge block to relationship working could be as complex as religious beliefs. One person thinks that God would be okay with polygamy. The other one is so traumatized by his past, he can't imagine sharing his partner with anyone and won't settle for anything but monogamy.

I have been in or have been close to all of these circumstances, and love just wasn't enough. Respect wasn't enough. Trying to create balance by give and take wasn't enough. Eating my words and swallowing my pride to accommodate my partner's truth, wasn't the answer. The only thing I came to was separation.

So, is love enough? *No* again.

> *Question: What makes for the best relationships?*
> *Answer: Mutual beliefs.*

You meet someone that is a part of your church or your political party. You begin a life that is based on something solid. You decide if the attraction is right. But the most important facet of the working relationship is: Are your dreams the same! A good look at how you would face life on a day-to-day basis is the way to discover if your love interest would be a good partner.

Things to ask:
- Do you usually brush your teeth before you kiss?
- Are you obsessed with cleanliness?

Finding Authentic You

- Are you obsessive compulsive about things in your life? What might those things be? (your car can't be touched, your things on your desk can't be changed around, don't try to take a sip out of the same glass as I drink from...)
- What kind of food do you like? (is one a vegan and the other a Brazilian carnivore?)
- Do you have to make the bed as soon as you get up?
- How many cups of coffee do you drink a day? Sometimes 5 cups of Starbuck can not only be a big expense, but can make a person crazy by midday?
- How do you spend your money—conservatively or frivolously?

You may be thinking to yourself, come on Bo, really?

Trust me, these menial things are the kinds of situations that break up great relationships. Then you add children to the mix and how each would raise a child, and the complications get worse.

Marriage and cohabitation is not something to take lightly. A great deal of these habits and dislikes above don't surface until you actually live with a person. Then life becomes a process of making concessions. No one wants to do that, especially as you get older.

So, is it any wonder that people of my age (middle-age) are staying single and can't find partners? I can see why and how often I share with my clients about the likelihood of finding that person who will fulfill this template. It's not an easy one to find.

So, if you really want relationship, what most of us do is settle. We look at the long list of things that our partner is and isn't and think: Is this something I can live with the rest of my life?

Maybe that's a good thing. Maybe this will help us

grow into more compassionate individuals and better people. I certainly hope so.

For the last years I have been on an adventure to find that right person. Wonderful men have come into my life and have had such great qualities. I love them all still. But there were ways I could see that our lives just wouldn't jive as we moved forward, so I moved on.

Sometimes I mourn in my heart for not having the fortitude for trying to work it out. Then most times I congratulate myself for respecting my wants and desires enough to move on, even though I loved big and without restraint.

Ultimately, you have to choose. As a wise person said to me, "It would be better to be in no relationship, than be with the wrong person."

Discovery 21: Getting Older

Turning one year older, you would think, would not be all that memorable after fifty. Something different and peculiar happened yesterday. I actually let go of trying to make the day special.

I coach people almost every day to let go of all things that no longer serve them and be willing to walk on a pathway led by Spirit—in the NOW, but sometimes I realize that I don't take my own advice.

Yesterday, my mom had invited a few friends and family over for a birthday celebration. I left the house to go out dancing without even cleaning up. I'm sitting here the next day with an entire porch left unclean. Leaving a mess for more than 24 hours is so not like me. I'm not even worried about when I'm going to clean it. Maybe it will clean itself!

I'm talking to the OCD, ADHD folks who have had an emotional life of disarray, so now everything in your physical life has to be in perfect order. Sometimes it's okay to let a little mess be with you, just to remind you that it's fine to be less than perfect.

I hope the rest of my life, I will leave little reminders all around me that say, "Bo, it's okay to be just who you are. People will love you and like you, even if you're not perfect!"

When I blew out my candles yesterday, I heard, "Speech. Speech!"

The only thing I could think to say was, "In all the time of my life, the one thing I have learned is that connecting with friends, loving and being loved is truly the only thing that brings joy to my heart."

This is wisdom.

Discovery 22: Walking the Path

My hands are typing, and yet my mind is completely still. I believe sincerely that even my own humanness sometimes inhibits me with depression, illness, a lackluster idea of the future, and mostly problems separating my human past with the absolute truth of the NOW. When I am on track, I see the truth as if it were perfectly clear 100% of the time. But, when I wake up feeling poorly and am hindered by my human flesh and bones, sometimes, it's as if I live in a fog that will not lift no matter how many prayers I prayer or how long I meditate.

I often forget that I am a spirit, living in a very dense, very heavy human body. My spiritual memories of times past in other forms and other bodies are that of peace. The maladies of my human body now are often just my spiritual memory reflecting on the perfect connection between my spiritual density and where I once dwelled as JUST spirit.

Here, on this earth, I am inclined to feel like a wanderer in a body that just does not fit or suit me. I am mostly uncomfortable in my skin. I am allergic to the ways around me. My body and my spirit seem to fight off that which does not serve me. If all of these attributes seem to fit you, you are simply dealing with the paradigm of your spiritual essence living in a human body for a reason, a purpose, that you chose before your time on this Earth. The only thought that you are able think to inhibit this uncomfortable feeling is: I am here for a greater purpose!

What might that purpose be?

Well, if you are spirit-driven and are on this Earth at this time, you are specifically here to bring positive energy to a planet that is on a path toward destruction. So, if you cannot figure out why you are so uncomfortable living every day on this Earth, with your job, the people around you, and especially in your human body, you can rest assured there is a greater reason for your being. You are here, on Earth, to lighten the load for those blind human beings who cannot see the destruction they cause.

How do we do this? Meditation is the absolute way we can connect to our spiritual body and download, as it were, enough positive energy to contribute to the change of the Earth in this time of vast reconfiguration on the planet.

Fear not, my beautiful spiritual friends. We are all feeling this uncomfortable pattern in our human state. But, we must get to our spiritual place in meditation as much as possible to keep our mind charged with spiritual positivity to give back to the planet.

When you hear something negative going on around you; this is the time to emit your positive charge into the universe. You are needed now, more than ever, as the world is evolving and changing in a vast and quick manner. We must collect our energy as light givers and work together to enhance the positive vibration of the planet to save it from its own demise.

Think on these things. Find others who believe the way you do. Form groups to meditate together. Find a prayer partner and use your powers together to think greater, more powerful thoughts for the world and for your own human paradigm. If you are not here to make change, then who is?

Discovery 23: Our Social Networking World—How Connected Are We?

How connected are the vast array of people today compared to thirty years ago, when we had no cell phones and computers? In my lifetime I have seen life speed up and glue people together from all over the world. What may happen from this acceleration of life and connectivity?

I turn my head daily and someone collides with me from my past via life, television, media, or some kind of social networking.

Nothing and no one feels disconnected from me. You know that when you think of someone, or you write a note to someone, they often send back a letter that says, "I was just thinking of you." How do you think that is possible without some sort of spiritual, social consciousness? I believe that the outer sources of social connection are just mirroring our inner source now.

Just as a thought or an idea becomes something material, this social networking is an outer mirror of what has been for thousands of years in the spiritual world. What we have always been able to do via spirituality, suddenly we are now able to do in the physical.

A few years ago I thought of a dear friend who I feared had passed on, because I had lost complete touch with him after I moved from New York. Disconnecting wasn't in Tim's nature. Twenty years later, I put his name in a search engine, and 500,000 results came up. I tried to think of any way I could make the search smaller.

I began to add things like his middle initial, his career, and his original hometown. Soon the results were down to 1000. I looked through 25 pages of results. His photo was on the 25th page, as he was teaching Music History at Escuola Di Musica in Italy.

Finding Authentic You

No contact information existed for him. So, I wrote a note in my best Italian to the music department explaining that I was a good friend who had lost contact. Soon, I got an e-mail back that said Tim would be calling me that day, and he was very excited to hear from me.

We talked for three hours and ran up a $300 phone bill, sharing the minutes. But I didn't care. I felt as if I had found a beautiful lost friend that I never imagined I would recover. This is as a result of our computer world.

I turn on the television or watch a movie and the same thing happens:

- Sitting on the panel for *So You Think You Can Dance* was Rob Marshall, a guy I took dance class with from 12th grade through college.
- I read an article in the NY Times about a woman I know who wrote a delicious new novel.
- I dated the actress Patricia Heaton a couple of times when I was 23.
- Every night when I watch Anderson Cooper, I think about hanging out with him in Nashville while he was here on a job. And, yes, he is a great kisser.
- The Voice of "The Little Mermaid" was my best friend in NYC.
- Holly Hunter was an acquaintance at Carnegie Mellon.
- I went to TPAC to see Dolly Parton's musical and the director of the show also took that same dance class with Rob Marshall and I in high school.
- I watched the final show of "Grey's Anatomy" last year and, David, someone I had a huge crush on in college was a doctor.

I have had similar experiences such as that in my life with other friends since *Facebook*. What a delight to hear from people who have changed their names and find you, when you couldn't find them.

Discovery 24: What? A Roach in My Kitchen?

When I lived in New York City in a five-floor walk-up on the first floor with radiators from the first century—the kind that pound when the hot water blasts through—you kind of expect roaches. Actually, if I were to have gotten up in the middle of the night and turned on a light in the kitchen about 100 water bugs and their sisters would have scattered at any given time, no matter how clean or remiss of food the kitchen had been. And mice, we had those, too. They had a little Dixie band that would get together on the top of the refrigerator right after my roommate and I fell asleep.

Today, when I see one roach, my whole body quivers. But then, it really wasn't such a big deal. I guess, at 21 and living in your own apartment in New York, I thought that I had just about made it. You know the saying, "If I can make it there, I can make it anywhere"? When you live in NYC at that age, I think *unstoppable* goes through your mind a lot, especially when mice are running across your feet and you bite into a roach wing in your fried eggs in the morning. EEESSH!

Growing up in the lower middle class helped me understand what the word *poor* meant. When I lived with my mother at the beginning of 11th grade, we had exactly $10 allotted for food each week. So, going to NYC and having to fend for myself on a little more than that was actually a treat. I remember the first week living there, I ate bacon sandwiches the entire week. I realized that was a luxury, so I switched to a steady diet of Ramen noodles, generic mac and cheese and boiled chicken thighs and legs. Yes, that was before my 21 years of vegetarianism.

I lived in Midtown, NYC, which is now quite posh and gentrified. When I lived on 49th Street and Ninth Avenue, drug pushers stood on every street corner and the apartments were filthy and practically unlivable.

One summer my neighbors were going away for three months. They had a really cool apartment, because the husband was a carpenter and remodeled the place. They asked me if I wanted to sublet. So, I did and subletted my own apartment across the hall. It turned out to be a moneymaking project.

I made more money subletting my own apartment than I did living in theirs. My neighbors just wanted someone whom they could trust in their apartment, so they charged me less, while I made a profit from subletting mine.

In the first week I just cleaned my neighbor's apartment. I remember scouring the living room area, which my apartment didn't have. But after I had cleaned everything to the bone, I noticed that the carpet moved by itself—literally. I had a couple friends with me, helping me. We were Pentecostal then and began to pray in tongues. We lifted up the carpet to find a myriad of roaches—cousins of second cousins crawling on top of each other boring into the wood floors.

How could my neighbors not have noticed thousands of roaches living under their carpet for God knows how long? We all actually screamed and ran to the store for some kind of industrial strength roach bomb. I stayed at a friend's for two days before I went to clean up the dead bugs.

The moral to this story is that no matter how much you clean the surface, you have got to look under things. Even in our minds, sometimes the surface appears happy and joyful, but often we hold deeply-seated fears and anger so far beneath the surface. To realize these emotions exists, you have to clean the surface, then sit quietly to see if your hair moves.

Discovery 25: When Is Enough, Enough?

After a tasteful watermelon and baby greens salad with a champagne vinaigrette dressing and a great steak dinner, I ate a large crème brulée for dessert. At the end of the meal, I had had enough to eat. I couldn't open my lips for one more bite, not even if the food were the best of the best or any kind of tasty treat. I had simply had enough.

A healthy body signals us when it has had enough food. If, perhaps, I would have eaten one more bite, I probably would have regurgitated. Some people, however, have stretched and stretched their stomachs so much that the appestat, which regulates our hunger, malfunctions. When this happens, a person can eat as much as he or she wants and never feels the pain of overeating physically. Mentally, however, the challenge to diet becomes an entirely different story.

When young children get abused over and over again, their functional boundaries change. When you can't protect yourself; when you are taught that you shouldn't honor your basic boundaries; you lose the sense of what is enough. You simply learn to tolerate until the abuse stops, if it stops. The result is Post-traumatic Stress Syndrome.

But the buck stops when children abuse their parents. This happens more and more when a child takes advantage of the loving nature of a parent and steals from them because of addiction. When this happens, enough can be measured. This abuse is, perhaps, the one time in all of these scenarios therapists and psychologists, alike, agree and say that codependency helps no one.

People don't learn lessons by others bailing them out of trouble. In fact, this kind of codependency can cause more dependency and worse addiction. The problem with this scenario is that the addict can't see through his own addiction to understand that he abuses the closest love that exists. They can see only one thing, the sickness and need for a drug of choice. Unfortunately, that does include the constant, consistent pain of the other person involved.

This scenario can cause a guilty need in the lives of a parent or lover who has striven to make good choice, but perhaps couldn't do the right thing all the time. I know of two parents who picked up their child from meth addiction so close to death and actually saved his life by a thread, when his partner left him, his friends abandoned him, and only they could have had enough love left to help.

This man has been drug free for four years and faithful and grateful to his parents ever since. Probably this is the first time in his life, he has understood his parent's unconditional love. He says he will never abuse it again. But even addicts who have been clean for twenty years fall sometimes. Addiction is an ongoing process of refusal to use ever minute of every day.

Will my friend stay drug free? Who knows? It's anybody's guess. Drugs are tough to beat, the hardest to beat. Is there a scenario in his life that will be too difficult to deal with and cause him to go back to what comforted him before? I sure hope not.

So, when exactly is enough, enough?

I'm going to take a leap of faith here and say that if you are doing your own spiritual work, you should be able to sense inside the leading of Spirit as to that decision. I want you to know that it is no one's business but yours what you choose for the sake of your loved one.

With all judgment out of it, I can still see why my sister stayed alone in Arizona waiting for her only child to get out of prison. It's not the best choice for her life, but her life isn't the only life at stake. I can make a great plan to fix her life and create health for her, if she were to let me, but it's not mine to fix. She and God are the only ones who know what's the right choice for her.

You see, I have learned one great lesson in life: I know when enough is enough. I am responsible for my path and my challenges. You are responsible for your path and your challenges. Where the two meet is only when you approve that I help. Even then, most times, codependency and love over-rides good sense. I know that, and I'm not offended by a choice that is not mine to make.

Discovery 26: The Murky Waters of the Mind

Nature often mirrors our lives. When I want to clear my koi pond of murky waters, I change the filter, vacuum the bottom of the pond, clean the pump, add chemicals that clear the water to kill molds and fungi that would create green muck. All of this together creates clean water for me to see my beautiful fish. Otherwise, I spend lots of money feeding koi and shubunkin that I never get to view, because they float on the bottom of the dirty pond, beautiful and expensive, but invisible to my eyes.

The metaphor here is that the fish are our spiritually-led thoughts. The pond is our mind. The murky, cloudy muck is the nature of life: sometimes—busy jobs, competitive thoughts, lusting minds, laziness, a crazy day with the kids, over-booking our lives, addictions, and anything else you can think of that will fill your mind with thoughts that don't quite serve the big purpose.

Each of these occupants of the brain facilitates murky water. The more you have in your mind, the cloudier it becomes. The cloudier your mind is, the harder it is to see and hear Spirit leading you to your peace and to your divine path. So, what is this metaphor that will clear the path to hearing God's voice:

Change the Filter. This can be likened to changing the part of your mind you listen to. There are two primary parts of the brain: the deductive and inductive thinking. The cloudy part tends to lean into the deductive, reasoning mind. The inductive mind is the observer, nonjudgemental part of the consciousness, the imagination and dreaming mind.

Vaccuum the Bottom. Clean up the messes in your mind. If old thoughts lay around in your mind unresolved, fix them! If you have unforgiveness in your life, do some forgiving. If you have a pile of papers on your desk, clean them up. Clutter makes a mess in your mind. Jobs left undone and decisions left undecided are just ways of keeping you from mental clarity. Fix this now! You are the only who can do it.

Add Chemicals. This can be likened to medications that may help with clarity. I'm on an antidepressant and have been for two decades. A small dosage is the difference between living a normal life and living a life like an animal stuck in a garbage can. Without this medication, my physical mind would be weak. I give my physical body a chemical to stop the obstruction of serotonin to the brain, which gives me a feeling of well-being, basically.

That being said, if you are bi-polar, and you expect to function in a world that will accept you, you better get on your meds. If you have ADHD and expect us to listen to your ramblings of three different topics with no breaths in between, you are probably not going to find that person. Get on your medication and stay on it consistently. They are meant to bring clarity to us and to you. No one will fault you for this clinical dependency.

Psychotropic medicine can help you, when taken in proper dosages. They rewire your brain to function in a normal pattern, so you can see clearly, think clearly, and manage life more easily. Don't make it harder for yourself in life, because you think you can be the strong one who can get along without your medication. You'll end up losing friends, jobs, and lots of life before you realize you just simply need to take one pill a day to function in a real world. Trust me, I've been through this many times. I've simply come to a place where I realize, like arthritic pain, I have to manage my own illness. My brain has a disease that can be treated fairly easily. But it will take my cooperation.

Discovery 27: Bored But Not Broken

I have a relative who had won every science award in high school. When he was five, he could recite adult monologues with definition and strength. Everyone thought he would grow up to be a genius. Today, he is in jail for theft, drug dealing, and possession.

When he is not in jail or in detox, he sits around all day pretending he is looking for a job. He's twenty-five and too old to be living at home with no job and no purpose, but his dependency on drugs makes him way too vulnerable to be alone.

I have a young client who can take a car apart, repaint it, weld any broken parts back together then reassemble it. She can't let go of her addiction to alcohol to give life a chance. In these young people are witnessing boredom or brokenness? Are we not encouraging them to take on enough responsibility to give them a reason to live past their addictions? Or are we simply acquiescing to their bad image of themselves and pouring our own negative belief about them into their vulnerable souls without even knowing it?

This is a lot to think about. Addiction boggles my mind. I have never seen so many good people fall prey to the sad, secret belief of the addict that there is no way out but the drug of choice: food, cigarettes, pot, crack, meth, Hydrocodone, Oxycontin, sex, porn, gambling, cocaine... the list goes on and on. I have also never seen so many people go so far into recovery and then blow it after six months, a year, or two years. I have even seen some fall after ten to twenty years of being clean.

Most therapists, even nonbelievers, can't look past the facts that most people who actually survive addiction are people who have a spiritual encounter and continue on a spiritual path, thereafter. I wonder if spirituality is the retreat from boredom the addictive brain needs. Think about it! What kind of brain functions on the external belief that something tangible will make it happy? The egocentric brain. Will that unhealthy ego brain ever be satisfied by anything on this earthly plain—truly satisfied?

I have had many successes in my life. I have lived many places. Loved many people. Nothing but God or a personal spiritual experience fills the gap of emptiness inside when I am alone and facing myself.

I don't want to exclude any religion or practice from this spiritual experience. Because when your spiritual breakthrough is real and authentic, you attain peace beyond understanding. So, don't be stymied by my insistence in calling my spiritual master God or any other name. Truth be told, I have come to meditate more like a Buddhist these days than any other form of religion.

> *Call it whatever you like, but simply call on it, seek it, believe in it—this spiritual belief will change your world forever.*

I went to a spiritual group meeting filled with mostly therapists and ministers. A minister friend spoke of people who inspired her into being a Methodist preacher. She pulled out a book from her bag called, *The Dark Night of the Soul* by Gerald May, which I read about ten years ago on a vacation. When she saved the book for last to speak about, I knew we had a kinship, because I could tell the book changed her as it had changed me. After reading the book, I suddenly understood why I had been through all the pain in my life. I found my power to move forward into my calling. As a result, whatever my addictions were, they disappeared without me even knowing it.

You see, stopping an addiction can't be the focus. Creating a new path toward something powerful that invites prosperity, enlightenment, truth, joy, empowerment, and an authentic drive in you toward the future is what transforms all that is negative in your life

Finding Authentic You

into something wonderful. You will have no need for your addiction, if you have joy and love and purpose.

This is a spiritual calling and transformation at its best.

Discovery 28: Fixing What's Not Broken

Most neuroscientists believe we use just about 10-20% of our brains. What about the rest of it? I experienced some chest pain a few months ago. I called my primary care physician at Vanderbilt. He said, "You should come in ASAP."

I went in the next morning for the earliest appointment. My regular doctor wasn't available, but his boss examined me. She took an EKG of my heart and said, "I don't want to alarm you, but in a minute or two, there is going to be a gurney in here to rush you to the emergency room. I believe you are having a heart attack!"

"Oh," I said, the sweat beads collecting formidably on my forehead. My mother had just been released from the hospital from a triple by-pass. "Really, God?"

So, after a battery of tests, a couple of very adorable doctors checking every orifice, ten hours of my life, and my family's and friends' worry, the doctors decided it must have been indigestion. Nothing broken, nothing fixed.

How many people *think* or *believe* they have some disease and really have nothing at all? How many doctors treat symptoms that essentially are imagined? I once had a parent bring in a child for hypnotherapy because of migraines. The child said that on a scale of 1 to 10 for pain, the migraines were a 10. He was 16 years old. His life stopped because of this problem. His mother wanted her child back. He had not been to school in a year.

But when I got him alone, he acted as if he had no pain at all. Now, I have had migraines at a pain level of 10, and I know how they made me feel. I couldn't have been talking to anyone. I would have been hulled up in bed with an ice pack on my head, in a dark room, with no sound, with heavy compression on my body, and riddled with lots of pain medication. He had made it very clear to me and to the therapist who sent him to me that this was psychosomatic.

Eventually, it was discovered that the mother was overbearing and trying to control the child, and she was the one who needed therapy, not him. When this evidence came to pass, the son's migraines suddenly went away.

Discovery 29: Reality or Fantasy

Fantasy: You come home from work and have had a rotten day. Your partner soothes you with warm, comforting words. You have all the attention you need to feel uplifted and secure. He runs a bubble bath for you, turns on your favorite music, and pours you a glass of your favorite wine. "Here, babe. Anything else I can do to make up for the shitty day you had?" You take the glass from him. He slips his arm around you and kisses you softly on the neck and whispers, "I love you so much."

Reality: You complain to a friend about your wife again. You have been together ten years with no children. You get so weary of the same argument that you, sometimes, just want to leave? But you remember something important you said to yourself just before you committed to this relationship, "I know this marriage is where I'm supposed to be. I've been in others, and there have been challenges there, too. I know that these challenges just mirror what I need to work on in myself. I will stay and see this through, trying to make every day better."

Which world would you rather live in?

Only a fool would say that he or she would rather live in reality. Reality just reeks sometimes. Reality tastes like boredom, impatience, and feels like the same moves with the same words, and even the same food cooked on the same days of the week. Yet, somehow most of us end up in relationships exactly like the reality above. Why is that?

Usually, our first relationship typically mirrors the relationship that we had with our most antagonistic parent. We choose a partner, unbeknownst to us, who is just like that parent. Once the great sex and romance goes away, we find ourselves in a battle that is exactly as we had with that parent, who never stopped poking us with small pricks of poisonous darts. Most of us tend to divorce or leave this pattern after a while.

We go on to another relationship. If we were lucky, we learned a bit about what isn't a healthy relationship. But three years down the road, we find ourselves in a similar situation. We begin to think that relationship is a scam, and everyone mirrors the same antagonistic parent dressed up in sheepskin waiting to attack.

We break-up and fly solo for awhile, date around, and maybe sleep around. None of the above fulfills us. Or maybe it does for a bit. But then, we get hungry for something more permanent.

We might see a therapist to assure us that we do not end up in the same, old relationship again. We get dictums and rules about what to watch out for. We do a lot better this time. But after the romance wears off, we still find ourselves struggling. Why?

Because of one simple fact: True, loving relationships are just mirrors for spiritual growth. If you're not ready for that, don't get in one. I used the words "true and loving" carefully, because I'm not suggesting you should ever stay in an abusive relationship.

Reality Check: I recently got into a live-in relationship after ten years of vowing I wouldn't do this again unless it was absolutely the right person. When I met my partner, everything about him yelled out: THIS IS THE ONE WHO WILL BE FAITHFUL AND LOVING FOR THE LONG HAUL!

Notice, I didn't say that everything about him said, we will never have a disagreement or have to learn to accept each other with all our baggage. And let me tell you, my darlings, after 53 years, I came with some heavy baggage. I feel lucky anyone would venture to pick up one of my suitcases, let alone want to co-abide with each one of them.

Relationship is more about a consistent and constant

commitment to stay together and to love with compassion, even when you can't understand or have trouble sleeping when they snore. Very few species on Earth mate for life. This is probably because there are so many alternatives to loving, committed relationships that actually give us some sense of peace and satisfaction. But for some of us, albeit, most of us, relationship is a part of being an adult.

As an adult, you realize that what a neighbor possesses isn't necessarily the best until you're living in his shoes and can see into every corner of his house.

Reality or Fantasy? I'll stick with Reality this time.

Finding Authentic You

Discovery 30: The Element of Surprise

When you read a good novel, objectively the writer want to create a page-turner. Each paragraph should lead you to the next, each page to the next page, each chapter should have you hungering for what is to follow. I wonder how much of this element of surprise we can bring into our own lives to make our days more interesting for all those participating, including you.

Today was a great example for me. My family had nothing planned for this holiday. My mother had bought some things to cookout on the grill. My partner and I thought maybe we would go away, but we decided against it. We actually had waited to see if the weather would cooperate with us going to our favorite short vacation spot, Beersheba Springs, Tennessee.

As time and the weekend would have it, neither of us took the initiative to make a plan. We woke up this morning with nothing scheduled. I didn't fret, as I may have done in the past. I sat and wrote my daily Discovery and let the rest of the world decide what to do.

I listened with one ear as I heard some planning going on between my mother and my partner. I heard them talk on the phone to a friend about joining us for the afternoon cookout.

When I finished my writing, I got a phone call from my best friend. I asked him what he was doing for the afternoon. He was free, so I invited him to come over. The day turned out to be wonderful.

We played fun games on my new 3-D television and ate great food. Then we laughed and carried on at the dinner table until everyone was tired and ready to *call it a day*.

It was an absolutely perfect and authentic day with no planning on my part and no fretting about the outcome. Every attribute of the day intricately knitted itself together as if it all were meant to be.

When I write novels and books, I never know what's going to happen next. I don't plan the entire outline as some writers do. I develop characters and situations, then I let the characters choose what's next. This style of writing is more exciting, because I don't know what's going to happen either. So, I figure that it would make for a better novel or book for a person reading, as well as fun for me.

In life, we tend to plan a great deal. More importantly, we get stuck in the probable outcome. Is it because we need to be in control, or because we simply don't know how to let life unfold before us in a natural way? I'm convinced, daily, that I should come prepared for life, but wait for the best to arrive.

That being said, sometimes I get an unction to call someone or make a date to meet someone for lunch. I think this, too, is Spirit's way of moving us forward. I know it's not my will, because it seems that the idea to meet or call flows from a different part of my brain or soul.

Also, I find that Spirit leaves signs when I need to spend time with someone. I might see his or her name somewhere. I may get a phone call. I may run into the friend some place unexpectedly. I know from these synchronistic events that I need to move my attention in his/her direction.

This is different than when I was younger. Then, I would want to *work the room*. I would see someone who could further my career and make a point in meeting and following up with lunch or dinner and a card—oh so many business cards. Everything then, now seems so contrived that it makes me feel almost dirty compared to the way my life unfolds more simply now.

Yes, there are plenty of things I would love to happen in my life. But I have realized that my timing isn't the

Universe's timing. I can force things to happen, but is it worth it at the risk of my peace and my authenticity?

My first novel became published because a friend urged me to go to a writers' conference just to spend time with her in Colorado Springs. I met my agent there and my publisher there. I recited a short story on the first day of the workshop. A publisher loved it and asked me to submit my work to her after the conference. It was one submission, and I got the deal.

Before that, I had sent out literally 100's of proposals with nothing to show for myself. Did I learn a lot from the old belief? Yes. But did I make a step forward toward my dream? No. Not until I answered the call of Spirit, did I actually move forward.

The next year, that same writer's conference was so impressed that I got an agent and a publisher at the last year's conference, the producers of the conference invited me back, all expenses paid, to be a presenter. As a presenter, I hung out with all the publishers, editors from big NYC and LA publishing companies and the agents. From that one spiritual move with my friend's call the year before, my entire writing career began.

Let God help unfold your dreams... with you. I assure you that you will be more at peace and more in line with what the universe has to offer and be more prepared for the reaping of your success than ever.

Discovery 31: The Answer to How Is Yes!

Sometimes you sit somewhere and listen to a person speak. An amazing quote that speaks directly to your heart wakes you up inside. My friend Jana Stanfield said this yesterday: The Answer to how is simply yes! When I heard her speak this, my eyes opened wide and breathed deeply. I definitely heard what was offered by Spirit and by Jana.

We spend our entire life thinking about how we will get to our dreams. Most of the time our internal mind says *no*, because... we don't have enough money, we are too old, we are overweight, we are too ugly, we have too many children, we need the money for the house. The answers become endless no*s*.

> *But what if we just said yes! and began from there?*

I remember a time when I had just $155 saved in the bank. I was twenty-one. I got a telephone call from a great friend and mentor, who passed on this year from cancer. He asked me if I would sublet his apartment in NYC for the summer, while he acted and directed at summer stock in Ohio. My dream as an actor/singer/dancer was to move to NYC and work on Broadway.

I didn't think the word *no*. I thought and said *yes* immediately to the call! NYC was my dream. I didn't care that I had only 155 dollars saved. I would figure something out. I would get the money before I had to leave. I would take the trip (even if I had to ride my bicycle) to get there. This is answering the call to a dream—perhaps, not the adult reasoning I would use now, but adventurous.

Finding Authentic You

As we get older, we tend to lose fearlessness. If I were faced with the same decision, today, I would probably say, I cannot afford to move with so little money. But I also have a house payment, $3000 worth of bills a month, a mom to take care of, a partner to consider, and a business that I have grown for years. Many things stand in the way of the *yes*. I get that. But still, sometimes our dreams aren't as big as moving our lives to NYC!

Sometimes dreams are just as simple as buying a pair of skis and taking that trip you have been wanting to take for three years, but you have been letting every other person and financial obligation stand in the way of it. What would it hurt to spend a little money on yourself and take five days off to ski and let your heart sing?

Isn't your soul worth it? I'm speaking to myself now. Because I'm the one who has snuck in a one-day ski trip in some hole-in-the-wall place like Paeoli Peaks, IN, every year, because I just can't seem to see clearly enough to give myself a true vacation. This year I said *yes* to a week-long Caribbean cruise! That's more like it!

One day isn't enough to get away and let your heart sore. You need the first couple days just to let go of your anxieties of work and separate from all the network of everyday chores to get to the place where your mind begins to explore the newness of freedom. I had that chance three years ago when I went to Key West and Miami for a week.

By the end of the week, I jet skied and took boat tours, and shopped like I truly enjoyed vacationing. I was carefree. I miss that part of me. We all need to experience letting go in our lives at least once a year, so that we can bring a little peace and joy back to our everyday lives.

So, the first thing I'm going to do when I get off of this computer is begin to envision my cruise. I don't care who doesn't want to go. I'm going to make it happen, and I'm going to have the time of my life. I deserve it, as you deserve to have the time of your life!

Say, yes, to your dreams today. We follow many things in life—Twitter, Facebook, YouTube, *Jersey Housewives,* sports... When nothing technological lured us, history records that people followed stars. For instance, the wise men from the New Testament followed the yonder star to find Jesus' birth. It's safe to say that the study of stars and the mapping of them to show the future was once something people used for direction, especially those with deep spiritual knowledge.

I find it interesting today how we manage to forget something as vast as the stars in the universe most nights, only to turn on the television or computer and look at YouTube and follow our friend's social computer lives, or worse yet, follow the lives of people we have no connection with or care about.

I looked up into the sky last night just before the sunset. The vast array of magnificent colors sprayed across my view. Even so, I watched for a minute and hurried inside to follow something I had DVR'd.

Life is not about simplicity anymore. If you think it is, than you have unwound from a very complex world and made it simple. When most people wake up, they start the day with news blaring, babies crying, traffic stifling, work pressuring, money issues, and relationship problems—to mention a few.

To live with no complexities, you would have to get a divorce, leave your children, get a job plowing fields in Montana on a farm far away from town, and, yet, still money problems might take away your peace.

Why did God, in this day and age, as opposed to all the thousands of years prior to our present-day lives, make life so fast-paced and unusually socially connected?

Everyone is a call or a click away. Even people in the farthest parts of the world can be contacted on Skype and called and spoken to with full vision. We are a world that is going somewhere quickly, faster every day. The question is where are we headed? If we follow prophetic order, we may look to someplace like the book of *Revelations* and speculate that these are the final days before something cataclysmic happens to change the earth and all the people in it. Most of the book of *Revelations* is a huge metaphor, so the interpretation of what that experience might be is certainly left up to us.

This is just a moment, a blip, perhaps, maybe even a dream of what's to come. We will be translated and changed. The evidence is all around us in the metaphors of the universe. Translated how? The answer to that is simply: *yes*!

Discovery 32: Who Am I Without Him/Her?

I asked my dear friend and forgiveness coach, Rev. Donna Michael if she had ever had clients who think about bad past relationships, then fantasize about being with that person, while living with their present mate. She answered, "All the time, but not because they want to be with their ex. We pine for the ones we leave, because we miss who WE WERE with that ex-partner!"

I think that is just about the most brilliant advice I've heard this month. In other words, I don't miss my exe, I miss the man I was with my exe.

- Perhaps, I was funnier with my exe, because he liked to laugh.
- Perhaps I talked more because he enjoyed a great glass of wine and conversation after dinner.
- Maybe I was sexually more involved because it mattered more then when I was younger.

All these things could be very possible, and still not make me want to actually be with my ex-partner.

When something becomes this clear, I breathe a sigh of relief. It's as if I have realized life, as I know it, will change just from one bright -aha- moment. You've got to love when the bright light of Spirit shines on you. I feel as if this advice will help many in the days to come.

I started making a list this evening of all the things that I missed about myself, from my first relationship to the last relationship that I had left. Here are some of the things I came up with:

- I spent more time socializing;

- I had a better work ethic because more of our time together was about work;

- I enjoyed spending more money, because we jointly had more money (or maybe as I look back, more desire to use credit);

- I enjoyed spending more time planning get-togethers, because socializing was an important part of our relationship;

- I spent more time vacationing, because I valued time off more than I do paying off my home;

- I spent more time talking about the arts and going to opera, the symphony in the park, the ballet, because we shared those interests;

- I spent a lot more time working on projects together or separately, which made me feel as if I was always working towards something greater, because he was a workaholic;

- I had my own hobbies like ice skating and swimming because I had to spend time by myself.

As I look at this list of qualities and actions I have let go of with old relationships, I have to wonder why. With divorce I have let go of parts of my personality as well. Releasing who we are for another person isn't a necessity for good relationship, especially, if we let go of time that we need by ourselves to nurture our souls with things that belong only to us.

Naturally, I'm likely to think that I miss parts of myself because I'm not with that other person. This is simply not the truth. Perhaps, I have relinquished parts of myself to forget the old relationship, because it hurt too badly to be around certain people, certain activities, and do certain behaviors, which remind me of the past.

But what is not true in this circumstance is that I have lost the power to regain any of these behaviors again. If I have done my work in disconnecting from the past and regaining my autonomy from old relationships, I should likely be able to continue doing anything on my list above, without feeling sadness about a lost relationship.

Finding Authentic You

Discovery 33: Stop, Look, Listen!

STOP: Something in your body or in your mind pleads with you to pause. A pain calls out, a headache, a death in the family, a job loss, an addiction, or a relationship problem. Something in your life today says to you, "Stop! I need your attention!"

I want you to focus in on this particular part of your life, right now, and decide what the message is. Nothing happens in your life without a purpose. So, what is the message? You are not meant to live with this struggle. So, figure out why this message calls to you, and, perhaps, the pain will disappear.

A psychological approach called Gestalt Therapy suggests that everything going on in your mind and body could become a *voice* for a problem that is hidden therein. If you were to imagine speaking to that problem as a person sitting across from you and ask it why it has come to you, it would tell you the reason.

In fact, Gestalt Therapists will act as the surrogate and play the role of your problem, asking questions and putting you in a hypnotic place to answer the questions.

One time I had a Gestalt therapist ask me a random question at a party. Are you hurting anywhere? I said, "Yes, my neck and shoulders are killing me right now."

She took me into a nearby room and described what she did as a therapist. I was into it and let her do her work. She took on the role of me as I took on the role of my shoulder pain.

Within minutes I was crying and telling her that I had to carry the burden of my entire family and relationship. The burden was way too heavy for me to shoulder. I needed to find a way to relieve some of the pressure. This information brought me to a new understanding of something I had no idea manifested in my life. I was grateful for her help, reaching out to someone she barely knew.

LOOK: The fast pace of life hardly gives us time to breathe, let alone have time to take a good look at what we're doing and how it's affecting our lives and, perhaps, the lives of our children and partners. We need to slow down to a pace that allows us to feel the pulse of the Earth. Yes, I said that. I know that is a little *woo woo* for some of you. But hear me out.

If you have a metronome or have a cell phone that can download a metronome app for 99 cents, do it. Then set it for 1 second per beat. Close your eyes and breath for 6 seconds in and 6 seconds out. This breathing rate will cause your blood pressure to slow. Don't let any seconds pass between inhales and exhales. Do this breathing exercise for 3-5 minutes with your eyes closed.

If you think some thoughts that are stressful, move your eyeballs from left to right and let the thoughts sweep away, like erasing any visions you have coming up as you breathe. This is a NLP, neuro-linguistic programming technique.

In biofeedback, this breath rate will bring your body back to your calmest heartbeat. When you get to calm, you'll notice that you are more sensitive to that which is going on around you. Your body becomes less tense, and your sensory perception heightened.

LISTEN: This is the hardest part for people who never stop—for people who always find themselves doing for everyone, but not taking care of themselves. I'm talking to you, who is overweight, because you eat to comfort yourself or smoke to comfort yourself, or drink to get to sleep at night because you are so depleted of life energy from your work and family that you have nothing left to comfort you. Yes. Listen—intently to the voice that says: you are important as well.

It's time to make better boundaries in your life and stop letting people walk all over you. It's time to take time for yourself and feel your passion for a minute for whatever you love.

Listen to your heart. Breathe from your heart. Breathe from every part of your body. Feel your mind descend from your brain stem and drop into other parts of your body. Your mind may think, generally, from your head, but your mind does not reside physically in your head. Your mind is your soul and, if you let it, the mind can move throughout your body.

Feel your mind in your heart and in your belly. Feel your mind in your chest as you take in strong breath. Let out all the toxic thoughts on your exhale and fill up with your passionate dreams in living color.

Discovery 34: Self-Soothing

I saw a recent picture today on *Facebook* of seven of the best friends in my lifetime laughing hysterically. The photo expressed love, community, and joy in every way. The only thing that remained missing in the picture was me. I hadn't been invited to the party. It still seems highly unlikely that I'll ever be told why.

I teach the many levels of forgiveness one can go through on this path. This betrayal of friendship was and is the most difficult I have ever had to go through concerning forgiving. Why? Because of the two friends that I thought still cared about me in the picture, one hasn't responded to any phone calls or e-mails in months. So, now it's down to one great friend out of seven who still cares enough to go the distance.

My thought is always, what exactly is being spread about me that keeps all these people so distant? Not only are they being distant, but completely unresponsive. If it were I, and they had done something that was worthy of this treatment, I would be calling and speaking my piece of mind. You can be sure of that.

But none of them will talk. They won't talk to the one friend left standing, either. This makes amending the problem impossible, which I think is their ultimate plan.

What makes all of this even more difficult is that two of the people in the picture are (1) my exe of eight years and (2) his new partner of seven and a half years. I'm pouring my heart out on the page here, and I'm not sure what God has in store for all of you. I hope it's as healing for me as it is for you. Let's try to *therapize* this. This process is also known as self-soothing or self-talk.

Your highest self would say, "A friend would come to you and explain what was wrong. None of these people are being a true friend. Do you really want unauthentic friends in your life?"

Finding Authentic You

To that end, my Ego brain would respond, "Absolutely not. I have many better friends, actually, as a result of letting go of these friends. My newer friends understand me in a more recent way, whereas, the old friends kind of expect the old Bo to appear. I love the people in my life now more because they honor me and are drawn to my life because of spirituality and an express interest in a deeper communication in loving and in life."

The next thing my highest self would ask is, "So, why do you grieve when you see this picture? What is the prevailing feeling?" Ego would respond, "Abandonment. Betrayal."

To which my highest self says, "Those are strong feelings. When was the first time you felt abandonment and betrayal?"

Ego would respond, "My mother left our family the summer of third grade. I didn't see her again until the summer of ninth grade."

So, the higher self would speak again, "You are really angry at your mother then?"

"No," Ego would respond. "I believe my mother and I have dealt with those issues."

"Then what else has happened in your life between now and then that has made you feel so abandoned?"

I think my Ego would be in tears by now. "Every person I have ever loved intimately has hurt me. They have murdered and desecrated love. Even some of my best friends have betrayed me. I don't trust love and I don't trust friendship to last! That is what I'm hurt about. Love is supposed to be pure and last forever. Isn't that what we're taught? And love has proven to be everything but steadfast in my life!"

"Bravo!" the life coach in me says. "You hit the nail on the head. Now, who would you say is responsible for inviting all these so-called friends into your life?"

"Me," Ego would respond timidly.

"If you had it to do over again, knowing what you know about each of these so-called friends, would you invite them into your life again? Or are they better off not being friends?"

"I can see that each of these old friends has been either unauthentic or caustic on some level, draining me of vital life energy." Ego begins to feel some relief now. "My friends are much truer now. They are more equally yoked and support me spiritually and mentally."

"So," the life coach in me says, "God has made some good choices for you, then, even when you couldn't make the hard choices of leaving some old, loving relationships that, maybe, just weren't helping you grow anymore? Can you let go of your grief now?"

Interestingly enough... I'm ready to.

In the above scenario you must play the role of both the Life Coach and the voice of your Ego. This is self-soothing at its best.

Finding Authentic You

Discovery 35: Belief, Passion, Desire—Action!

A dear friend and I were talking today about getting busy with life. We have been playing with getting our acts together for so long. Now, finally, it's time to take this act on the road.

As we spoke, I said the most authentic words I had said all day, "If we truly wanted to be doing something, we would be doing it!" By that, I mean, I don't have any problem making things happen when I know I want them.

When I want to go on a ski trip, I make plans for it. When I want to compose a Discovery every day, I do it. When I contemplate about writing a new book, it doesn't get done until I'm absolutely passionate about the idea and desire the outcome with all my heart.

> *So, the ingredients to action are—belief, passion, and desire. If you don't have all three ingredients, there will be no steadfast work toward a wonderful result.*

I know this from many projects left undone and many completed. In seven years I wrote five novels. Only someone who is absolutely passionate about getting a novel published can write, edit, and complete five novels in that short time.

I'm sure there are more prolific writers than I, but I'm talking about novice writers—people who are just beginning to understand what it takes to be a successful writer. I went to every writers' conference I could find. I saved all my money for vacations that only including some kind of writing endeavor. I used my time and effort for my passion.

When I realized that I had spent the time that most people would have used to make millions on writing five novels, which have made their semi-permanent home in a nested folder on my computer; I decided that, perhaps, it just wasn't my time, or I wasn't writing work that appealed to the general public. I find it hard to be critical of my own work, even if I was a professional editor for fifteen years. The end result is telling, after all.

I went through the same passionate beginning in the acting business. I moved to New York soon after college. I didn't care that all I had only saved $400 and had a place to stay for just three months. I knew I could get a job and find an apartment, because I had faith in life and my passion. I did get work soon after I moved to New York and got my Actor's Equity card on my third audition—something that doesn't happen to most people. But I didn't question for a minute that I was supposed to be there and be on stage.

Passion and belief for a long period of time and with luck may end up getting you what you really want—fame and fortune; but, trust me, I have had friends in New York gain minimal success since I left. They have been there for over thirty years. Yet, they stay there because that is what they have chosen and desire. Now, it seems, I question most things that happens in my life.

Life comes down to: Is my passion greater than my desire to be comfortable at home doing what comes naturally? Early on, I had thought that passion meant fame and fortunate. Now, I absolutely know success simply means peace and happiness in the end.

Discovery 36: Letting Go

I sat at the movies watching *Silver Linings Playlist*, an Oscar winner in 2013, and suddenly my heart began to pound out of my chest. I felt as if all the doors in the theater were being locked. I was transported back to a time in my life when my father was drunkenly beating up my brother to a pulp. I lay on the top bunk for a half of the scenario. Then I jumped out of bed and ran to the neighbor's house for help.

During the movie, I watched from an observer's perspective as my entire body seized with pain and anxiety in the theater as the subject of the movie was exactly my childhood. I had to leave the theater or I would have curled up in a ball and cried like a baby. PTSD had hit me hard.

This, however, was the first time in my life I had really been able to watch PTSD happen from an observer perspective, thanks to all the meditating I do. Maybe, because I understood what was going on, the experience hit me harder than I had ever remembered.

I left the theater and proceeded to drive home, which I don't recommend. In my car, I called a therapist friend as I drove (another bad decision). After fifteen minutes of my friend talking me down from the bridge, I realized I was driving in the wrong direction. I had been disoriented enough that I didn't even know where home was. I ended up ten minutes from Columbia, TN, going in the complete opposite direction, an hour away from my home.

Since then, I have had a few PTSD moments. A couple of them have happened during the night. A dream sparked some terrible anxiety in me. I had to get up, do some EMDR exercises and meditate before I was able to get back to sleep.

Can you release something that your body and mind

doesn't want to let go of? This is a question I have asked myself many times. I believe that whatever anxiety or stress is holding on like glue, will someday—with clear, empowered belief and therapy—will be released.

Now I am seeing what is happening *as it happens.* I had never understood why I would act out of character sometimes and get cold and withdrawn. Now, I'm perfectly aware—so, aware, that I can ask my partner to help me as these emotions begin to surface.

Great relationships are wonderful when someone is compassionate enough to help you work through some deep issues. I suspect that God intended for us to work out most of our deepest relationship issues with our life partner, because he or she understands us in a way no one else does or would care to.

If you deal with this kind of stronghold such as PTSD, I recommend starting with some therapy. Many practitioners of all kinds exist to help people with disabling problems.

Choose the modality you feel is right for you by doing Google searches and seeing what therapy best suits your problem. For me, Hypnosis and EMDR, which are very similar modalities are the most effective when it comes to PTSD. In fact, a great deal of my family therapists and social worker therapists are using hypnotic techniques to uncover deeply seated fear and anxiety with *Parts Therapy*, breathing exercises, and Regression techniques, all specifically developed using hypnosis.

Discovery 37: The Secret to a Successful Relationship

Many people have asked me this question since I wrote my book "Your Gay Friend's Guide to Understanding Men." The answer is simple: Be as authentic as you can, the best person you can, and you will attract the best person for you.

I had a client recently who told me that he had trouble finding a girlfriend. He came from a small town. He felt like he had met all the women in the town and none were right for him. He had a special problem, though. He had trouble communicating his feelings and making conversation. He had more than one woman accuse him of complacency, *when the truth was*: he simply was too afraid to say what he felt.

After careful examination, we discovered that his mother was completely critical of everything he did and said. She had something to say about everything he wore, the way he fixed his hair, and especially about the different women he dated.

Since his mother was the first template of relationship as he attached to life, he imagined that all women were going to be like his mother. To find right relationship when you deal with an attachment issue such as his, you have to first work out your issues with a therapist.

There are many kinds of therapy that can help:
- clinical therapy,
- psychiatry,
- hypnosis,
- EMDR,
- Neuro-Linguistic Programming (NLP),
- healing touch,

- sound therapy,
- acupuncture
- aroma therapy,
- Reiki, and
- many massage techniques.

All of the above are different modalities and may resonate with you specifically on some level. For me, I had to try a few different types of therapy before I settled on acupuncture and hypnosis. As I do self-hypnosis every day and meditation, I combine the ancient modality of acupuncture or my daily meditation to find a holistic approach to my own healing—body, mind and spirit.

I noticed that the more energy I put into making my own life healthy, the better the relationships are in my life. I also noticed that I am letting go of old behavior, such as attracting people who were more takers than givers.

Now, my life is filled with great relationships of all kind, especially people with compassion and giving hearts. But I had to reach out to find these relationships. I meet most of my friends at a Spiritual Center I attend. I also go online. I go out to parties. I joined social groups. I am active in all social media. And I make a point to meet a new person almost every day, no matter if it's the mailman. The more people you connect with, the better you will be at opening your heart to socialization.

As a young person, I imagined that I would always be the person on the far edge of the couch at a party, sitting by a dim lamp, waiting in the mayhem for someone to find me. I never wanted to be the one who initiated a conversation.

Then I realized, when I took the reigns of my life and began to socialize and meet people, the process of building relationships became easier and easier. Now, I know literally thousands of people. Sure, they are mostly acquaintances, but most of them know my name and I probably know theirs. I feel great when I go to the mall or for a walk and meet someone I've encountered before, or has been a client, or has taken one of my classes, or has been in one of the churches in which I've ministered. I feel connected to life in a rich and organic way.

So, finding yourself is a big part of finding relationship, because your relationship with yourself is the first real, authentic relationship you build on your own. When you get strong and healthy and know what you want in a good relationship, I promise, if you make an effort, it will show up in your life.

That is not to say that relationships won't take work. They do. And that is also not to say that you may have to endure a few bad relationships to know what you want. You may do just that. In fact, probably so. That is also not say that you may have to know "exactly" what you want, or else you may end up with a slightly less refined version of your dream. All of these things are necessary in creating the reality of a good relationship.

Once the relationship is established, it also takes a daily dose of water (love, compassion, honor, and attention) to keep it blooming and healthy. Anyone who is in a well-developed relationship will tell you that intimacy does not thrive if it is left to take care for itself.

Discovery 38: Are You Really Asking for What You Want?

I asked a client this question: What do you really see yourself doing in a couple years? He said, "Well, I'm not sure. What I would love to do and what I want to do are two different things."

Talk about an ambivalent dream for the future. If you don't know what you want and desire, don't expect to see it expressed in your life. *What you are in mind expresses in kind!* What you believe about yourself and about your life will express itself one way or another.

One negative thought about yourself will exponentially empower itself and leave you in a negative place for a long time. There is also that 95% of human life that happens, and we have little to no control over it.

My lawnmower broke this morning on the week that my sisters are coming into town. My partner and I are staying at his house while my sisters and children are going to stay in my room and in the spare bedroom to save money.

We went to my partner's last night and the air conditioning was broken. There is absolutely nothing we can do about something strange like that happening. On top of that, not one, not two, but four of my Koi fish got caught in the net that was protecting them from the gray heron. They died in the heat yesterday before I had a chance to notice. Another 260 dollars lost on fish.

I'm not sure what Spirit is trying to tell me, but let me tell you, my ear is tuned toward heaven. I don't want or need anything else negative to happen. I've prayed, my partner and I have prayed together, let go, and now it's God's turn to help.

I'm not one of those spiritual advisors and clinicians who makes life entirely your responsibility. I know too well from the first three months of this year that you can be doing everything right and be directly in the middle of a wind tunnel that sucks your roof off, breaks your car, and all the other appliances and plumbing in your house to the tune of $23K.

I was hit hard. But, I didn't stop believing in the good that is all around me and is possible for me everyday. In fact, I put more energy into seeing and believing in my good.

I recited mantras, saw visions of gold raining down on me, and asked every spiritual friend I knew to pray "with me" as I believed for the good that God gives. (I'm not saying that occasionally I got disheartened. I did. But I tried very hard to believe the truth everyday.)

You may ask, isn't it a little bit prideful to ask for wealth and health when people are dying for no reason and poor exists all over the world? I would have to answer a hardy *no*!

You playing small in this world doesn't help anyone. In fact, if you have money, you can help others. If you stay poor and desperate, you are the exact ones that people have to help. What kind of energy is that giving the world? You are a child of God! Act like it.

> *If God, your creator, has all the wealth in the kingdom, shouldn't you be an heir to that wealth? I am not afraid to feel that.*

You are made in the image of God. God is perfectly healthy, is unlimited good, and is a creator. Are you playing small just so others won't perceive you as an Egotist?

I have a friend Sharon who is a CPA. Every time someone asks her what she does for a living, she says she's an accountant. She happens to be looking for another job. She told me she doesn't want to sound like an Egotist by flaunting her accolades.

I posed this question: What if someone you talk to has the capacity to hire a CPA and is looking for someone who has all your qualities? You may just miss the opportunity because you were afraid to say what you are. That advice changed her mind.

I heard her yesterday introduce herself as a CPA.

Discovery 39: Dragonfly

Not many insects, birds, or animals are able to see and fly in all six directions. The agile and beautiful dragonfly is able to do it all. Plus, its opal-like body seems to shimmer as it flies, making it look iridescent.

The dragonfly effortlessly flies, flapping its wings only 40 times a minutes compared to most insects, which flap at 600-1000 times. Dragonfly is able to achieve this power because each flap of the dragonfly's wings is 20 times stronger than insects and other birds.

The dragonfly lives most of its life unable to fly in the nymph or larva stage. It flies for only a fraction of its life, no more than a few months.

Yesterday, three dragonflies crossed my path—two while I was in my driveway admiring the flowers and pond and one landed directly on my windshield as I was driving. Of course, I am a believer that nature is constantly sharing with us its magical message.

The metaphor of dragonfly is a beautiful one. In most cultures *dragonfly* symbolizes the kind of change that has its source in emotional and mental maturity. It represents the deeper meaning of life.

Perhaps, as dragonfly passed me three separate times yesterday, it was saying, "Dig even deeper, Bo—gaze into the magnifying glass of life and see a richer purpose and reason for your life!"

Dragonfly is generally associated with being around water. Its ability to glide quickly across water reminds us to look beyond the surface of every situation. Its ability to see in every direction symbolizes power and omniscience—something that comes with spiritual maturity.

When we are able to be the observer of our own humanity, we rise above the two-dimensional life that only human eyes looking forward can visualize. When we grow spiritually, we expand our vision to multi-faceted, multi-dimensional life, which gives us a greater, deeper vision of all that is in our physical and mental path and beyond. This mental acuity comes with the practice of meditation.

Dragonfly can fly at 45 miles per hour. It can hover in one place, move up and down, side to side, and from front to back. It does all this with the elegance of a dancer.

Symbolically, this could mean that the more spiritually evolved we become, the gentler our steps appear. When you watch a ballet dancer glide across the floor, the objective is to see simplicity and ease when she dances; though it may have taken years of strengthening her feet and legs, and many falls to develop her poise.

Dragonfly teaches us that what takes most people years, can take a spiritually-led person half the time. This is because with divine inspiration, it is as if time has no bearing on the outcome. What is to happen through us— as God lives and breathes as us—now happens with the inspiration of Spirit and with the power of angels.

Dragonfly's magical iridescent properties makes it appear different in any direction you view it. This symbolizes our ability to become all things to all people, if need be. Dragonfly's character to change identity with each glance gives us the reality that our humanity is just an opalescent shell. Our appearance can change depending on who is watching whom and from what point of view you are being watched.

Lastly, since the dragonfly lives most of its life as a nymph or larva and spends just a few months of its life flying, we see that our mature spirit may not have as much time as we imagined on this Earth. We must accomplish our purpose and intention before our time on earth vanishes. With this knowledge, we become completely uninhibited, which makes us fearless in the face of human struggle. This last attribute of the dragonfly means the most, as it signifies to live each moment as it appears. The message of most sages in this time definitely is to live in the Now.

Discovery 40: Every Moment with You Is a Gift

Often we find it easier to give than to receive. Most people prefer giving, especially if they have been caregivers their entire lives. However, selfish or narcissistic people tend to find partners who prefer to give, so that they can take freely without the need to reciprocate.

As a practitioner, I have noticed that people who are nurses, caregivers, doctors, and mothers—to name a few—tend to take care of everyone else, first, instead of caring for themselves at all. "Make sure you put your oxygen mask on first, before you attend to your children."

A very good reason exists for this. If you have no air and can't breathe, you will have no chance of saving anyone else. Yet, even though we understand this concept in the friendly skies, we still may have trouble realizing that our self needs our not *selfish* at all.

Self-care is important because, if you are not happy and healthy, then you will have no energy to help others in your life. If you are one who will not take this advice, I bet you have an addiction, such as overeating or cigarette smoking or drinking alcohol in excess.

You do not need a brain surgeon to know this, if you don't get your needs met in any relationship—even relationships with your children, you are going to find a way of self-satisfying, even though that habit may lead to your own demise.

> *The gift moments I refer to in the title of this Discovery are the moments you spend with yourself.*

Are you taking the gift of time away, spa days, self-soothing, taking a fun class, going out with friends, reading a great book, and more specifically, meditation and spiritual seeking? If you take time to nurture yourself and find satisfaction and peace in your life, everyone in your world benefits.

- The happier I am, the more I enjoy my work.
- The more I enjoy my work, the more my clients benefit.
- The more at peace I am, the better I digest my food.
- The better I digest my food, the more my body uses the vitamins gleaned from it to provide physical health and strength.
- The more I laugh, the least likely I am to have a headache or body pain.

Self-care can lead to:
- weight loss,
- muscle growth,
- a new look,
- a better outlook,
- a loss of depression, and
- less of a need for multiple medications.

All of this leads to a better self-image. When you believe you are worth something great, then you make more money, attract better friends, and invite joy into every part of your life.

This also leads to ease in receiving from others. I look forward to my birthday every year, because I love getting gifts now. I see every present as a way for me to see my worth through other people's eyes. Everything from homemade cards to expensive baubles are all fair game.

As you read the last paragraph, if you were thinking: he sounds like he is selfish, because he loves to get birthday gifts. Is this not the thought of a person reared to believe that giving is the only righteous act on Earth?

> *Receiving gives someone else a chance at feeling that great joy of giving. If there were no one to receive, then none of us would have a chance to give.*

I'm not saying that you should expect a return from anyone. I'm implying exactly the opposite. Our gifts often come from other sources as we extend our hearts to unlimited giving.

> *The universal law of reciprocity would see to it that all of our needs are met as we give. It is law that we receive what we need, when we give.*

So, open your arms and get ready for the gifts that abundant, all-loving and all-giving Spirit is ready to pour out on you today. Imagine that someone is knocking at your door now holding that 20 Million dollar jackpot check. Imagine how your heart would feel if that actually were true.

Discovery 41: Finding Your True Purpose

Most of us spend our entire lives working, making enough money to pay the bills, supporting the children, paying the rent, making money for food, and satisfying personal needs; yet, very few of us truly find our purpose in life. Only 20% of us find a job that really brings joy to our hearts and lives daily. The Business Insider online says that in 2010, 80% of people *hated* their jobs—not just disliked—*hated*! How can that be?

I had a client who had aspirations of being a country singer and songwriter. He came to Nashville, met a woman simultaneously, ended up getting married. Soon after, his wife became pregnant. He began writing and working a part-time job, while his naïve wife told him she would work, while he pursued his dream. Soon, of course, she was unable to work because of the infant. They couldn't afford daycare. He ended forced to take a job in construction, he didn't really enjoy.

He especially hated the job when it would rain, and he would have no income for the day. The job would be postponed because of weather. It was now essential he came home with a certain amount of money, as he had the responsibility of child and wife and a home. To make the matters worse, in the next three years, the couple had two more children—unplanned.

Now he had to step up his game and create a construction company of his own. He then worked 10-12-hour days, six days a week, and hadn't written a song or had sung a song in four years. He was depressed and could barely get out of bed in the morning. But when three children jumped on top of him and screamed, "Daddy, Daddy, I'm hungry!" and Mom had left because of Dad's depression, there was little to do but get up and spend the rest of the day being the dutiful father.

This man now has the money for daycare, but really no

time to even enjoy his children. He wants his life back and wants a job that brings joy to his life. I certainly understand, but wonder exactly what a life coach can do at this point in the game. I suggested carving out time just for him. He looked at me with a quizzical stare. Really? When? Where?

I asked if he had someone he could trust to run the business for him, when he wasn't in charge. He, again, looked at me like I was a crazy man. I told him the first order of business, then, was to begin to farm out some of his responsibilities to people he trusted. He had to find someone he could hire to help him; otherwise, he could never get out from under the water.

He was drowning. So, after the first week, he interviewed a few people, and discovered that one of his cousins was interested in helping out one day a week for extra money. I told him to pay his cousin a fair wage and to take the day off. Keep the children in daycare or school. Use the day to write music or watch television or just sleep. He took my advice, wasn't out that much money, and actually enjoyed one day of fun.

The next week he began to look forward to the time off. Soon, he was making plans to write with old songwriter friends. Eventually, he did get a song on a major artist's album, which led him to be able to take two days off a week. Then, he got a few more cuts on albums. Soon he sold his construction business to his cousin and now writes music fulltime.

You have to make a plan and stick to it to get what you need out of life. There are ways. Yes, you may have to sacrifice the BMW for a couple of years. Trust me, you will be much happier driving the Honda to art class than you will the BMW, if art is what your soul desires. We are made in the image of Creator God.

That means, we all have the deep desire to create something special from our lives. We have Spiritual DNA that is compassionate, loving, prosperous, and all-

Finding Authentic You

knowing. Within each of us is not only the desire to find purpose, but the will to get it done at any cost. Find that power within you. It may be buried deep inside your 100 personal daily duties. But it's there.

Discovery 42: We Can Be One Two-gether

When a person thinks about being one with someone, he/she usually imagines that person being his/her mate. When a person imagines togetherness, we often think about family and the tight bonds that blood brings. But when any two people develop an intimate connection, in essence, we actually *rediscover* our oneness with that person. We have always been One with everyone. The physical body causes separation, *The Course of Miracle* says, which makes all of us on Earth feel as if we are separate. But, we are all One in God.

If you believe that we were all together with God before the worlds were formed, then, at one point outside of time, all spirits were merged with God. If this were true, then what we experience as separateness and segregation is really an illusion based on human principles and beliefs. The truth about all that exists is truly unity.

When spirit comes into body, it individuates. Every individual has a separate body and a unique personality or Ego. But what happens when we close our eyes and gather in a circle? At the center of everyone involved is one exponentially large vision. It seems that the Ego self merges into the larger Unified Self, which increases as people gather with the same purpose.

I believe when Jesus said that "where two or more are gathered, there I am," He was considering the power of the Unified Mind. This would be like taking a crystal and shattering it. Each individual shard would be beautiful in its own right, but if parts of the whole connected together to reunite, more magnificence and power would be displayed—especially, if we consider the power and ability for crystal to hold memory and to refract light.

A secret exists in the thought of unity. An entire religion is called Unity, based on practical Christian principles. In fact, Unity's originator, Charles Fillmore, called it Practical Christianity. This religion has a very close cousins—The Centers of Spiritual Living. Both religions came as a result of a small group of spiritual visionaries studying together in the late 1800s. Out of this group splintered the two larges churches and various smaller fractions, which all have similar beliefs. Practical Christianity or New Thought is basically an idea that the bible has more than a literal meaning. In fact, parables in the bible have strong metaphoric meaning as do the lives and stories of the bible's characters going all the way back to Adam and Eve.

Meta- means *out from*. So, believing in metaphysical principles of the Bible would mean that you literally lift yourself out from the original meaning and strive for deeper and more experiential meaning.

I used to be a Pentecostal preacher who believed in the literal and only literal meaning of the Bible. But even then, I was always searching in the *Lexicon* and *Concordance* (study books for ministers) for other meanings and translations because I would tend to come up empty when comparing the scriptures with my personal belief.

I think that almost every preacher or biblical scholar initially begins his/her study to prove a point outside of tradition. I wanted to believe that God was bigger and more loving than I was taught as a young Christian. I wanted to believe that God had a better plan that heaven and hell, and as a Catholic for a time—purgatory. As a result, I left religion for a while to study on my own.

I realized that almost every religion had its unifying beliefs. At their core were very similar desires—to love, to unite, to heal, to give, to dwell in peace, and to gain compassion. No matter what religion you choose, there is one commonality—the idea of unity.

When two or more are gathered in one belief, they create power. Some have proven over the years that power can be dominated by Egotism and transform undeniable belief into evil and death.

Finding one's own *authentic* belief should precede unifying with others. Even then, I believe there will come times when you need to reach out to another belief or go inside to dig deeper where only God dwells solely with you. Either way, your spiritual walk is based on your oneness with others and a total commitment to finding your deepest commitment to life, your brothers and sisters, and what you call the Eternal One.

Discovery 43: Raise Your Self-Worth

All those who don't believe you can achieve what you set out to do, stomp your feet! Wow! I think I feel the earth moving under my feet. Most of us have negative energy around our belief.

I had a conversation with a good friend. We were talking about not doing what you have committed to do and how it affects your self-esteem. I have always been taught that the psychological ramifications of "not doing what you set out to do" affect your self-esteem more than you know.

By going against your own will, you set your self on a course of not trusting your *own* intentions. If you don't trust yourself, this makes it very hard to trust someone else.

I know that if I have an intention for the day and don't accomplish it, I feel as if I have dishonored myself and my time. If I had no choice in the matter—for example, an emergency hospital visit—I wouldn't feel this way. However, if I had chosen to do something else besides what I had set out to do, my anxiety about the chore would build up.

Sometimes the energy of stress around "not doing something" gets so bad, that it becomes anxiety. This anxiety can build a wall around the very accomplishment you set out to achieve. This means that in the subconscious you have built a trigger to be upset around the idea of finishing what you started.

An underlying animosity toward myself also happens when I look in the mirror and see 10 pounds I don't want to have hanging over my belt. If I keep saying, "Today is the day of my diet," and I choose to eat cake and cookies and candy again (because someone brought them home), I don't feel good about myself.

This consistent *anti-behavior* can't help but affect my

self-worth. Though I joke about it, life becomes more difficult if I have someone living with me who frequently eats sweets and carbs, and I'm trying to avoid them. I find it very difficult to avoid what is directly in front of me.

Most of our intentions have to do with habit breaking, but other than ill-begotten intentions, there are plenty of actions in our lives we set out to do—a book we want to write, a class we want to take, a paper we need to finish, a room that needs painting—but we never complete. A person in the world doesn't exist who hasn't, at one time, had trouble accomplishing something. This is normal. But, when you see almost everything in your life is half-finished, you know you have an issue with self-esteem and a psychological problem attaching itself to the word *complete*.

Perhaps, it's an anxious feeling; maybe an avoidant feeling. But you can be assured it is a neuropathic pathway that is settling for less than you deserve. You may have to become the dreaded parent in your own life and treat yourself with a strong arm of intent. By this, I mean that your subjective, observer mind must communicate with your objective mind as if it were a parent to a child. Here is a prayer for you to say around this matter:

> *I know now that I am creating a pathway to truth for myself and for my projects that will lead me to perfect completion. As a result, my self-worth has becoming the true me that Spirit intended it to be. And so it is.*

Discovery 44: Limitless Self-Worth with Surrender

A friend sent a link to a blog about a man's story discovering his dear friend and brother was gay. Instead of feeling compassion, I became antsy and frustrated while reading. The story was based on a small town's point of view aband clothes). Small town, small minded—I believe I understood the premise and the metaphor.

The author talked of his brother having no friends, though, and being in the closet, because of the few people his brother confessed had rejected him. The gay man decided not to tell anyone else of his sexual preference.

At this point, I understood his dilemma. The gay man wasn't living up to his Authentic Self. I couldn't find compassion for him, because the gay man hid from the person he was and wanted to be. How could he expect anyone to love him when he hated himself?

> *If you are gay, bisexual, or different in some way, you can't expect any of us to love you and your differences if you don't fully accept yourself. Start from this truth.*

I understand that some people have religious beliefs that cause a major block to accepting themselves. Not one ethical psychology book exists that even suggests that being gay or bisexual is a choice. In fact, plenty of theories exist that being gay may be genetic. So, just release yourself from that old story now!

If you still have a problem with believing that God is upset with you for being the human he created you to be, you need a different approach to spirituality and a new face for God.

What compassionate human parent would throw away

a child because she was different? Certainly, we can attribute more compassion to an all-loving God.

The other problem with the story about the gay man was that I actually can understand the premise of friends rejecting him on the basis that he had been lying to them for a long time about his sexuality. Lies, in my book, are huge and relate to trust issues. If I can't trust a friend, he simply isn't my friend.

Sometimes being abandoned by a friend or family member after coming out is not because you are gay. The friend may release you because he or she doesn't know who you are now—as you have been hiding your true self from him/her for so long. They feel betrayed.

There are two sides to the coming out story. The person making the change and finally having the courage to come out is responsible for having compassion for those whom he tells. I'm not saying you shouldn't expect respect from parents and family members, who have a certain sense of fairness and the need to accept you, which is built into the familial process.

However, in friendship, you can't expect that same premise. Friendship is based on trust and knowing someone intimately. If I had a friend who was straight for a long time and suddenly decided he would finally tell me he was gay—even though I may have suspected—I may be a bit put off by him. As someone with a lot of compassion about this particular situation, I would certainly not reject the friend, but encourage him to find himself. However, not everyone is as understanding.

If you tell a friend about a change in your life, such as: "I've decided I'm going to have a sex change. I really want to be a woman!" Can you expect that old friend to not be befuddled and confused?

You may think: But I knew you. I undressed in front of you. I feel lied to. Those are probably the feelings you should expect with your truth. I would feel fortunate if the person understood at all.

If he or she didn't, I'd simply have to move on and find someone who did love me for who I am. This is the hardcore truth of love and friendship. A hard lesson, yes, but a good one!

When you surrender to what is, accept what is, and move on from your dilemma—intelligently and with respect for yourself and others—you gain an unlimited amount of Self-Worth, no matter what the situation or change in your life. Authenticity is always the goal!

Discovery 45: Not Easy—But Powerful

How do you get rid of the trauma of rejection? She shared that it follows her and plagues her mind most days.

I have to deal with the same kind of Post Traumatic Syndrome Disease (PTSD) and Attachment Disorder. In fact, if anything has plagued me my entire life, it has been the FEAR of rejection. Fear is an acronym for False Evidence Appearing Real.

Nothing in life can hurt as bad as rejection if you have been wounded as a child, except, of course, *the fear of rejection*. Anticipating that which we believe will happen, often brings more anxiety than the rejection itself.

In one case, recently, in my life, I had sent out three emails and left two voice messages to a business associate. A week went by with no answers to any of them. I had the feeling of impending doom hit about midweek. "She doesn't like me anymore. She doesn't want to work with me anymore. I'm not talented enough, handsome enough, basically, good enough to keep her attention."

In this case I used Self Inquiry. The initial idea about self-inquiry is the recognition that we have more than one character living in our heads, or more than one perspective to view our thought process. Some thoughts, especially deep-seated wounds, act as if they have a voice of their own. These voices respond, they shout at you, and often they make you sad and depressed with their self-deprecating words. You can come into agreement with me about this multi-voiced being living in our brains if you simply ask yourself, "Who is speaking?" when you hear a critical remark in your mind.

I know this voice certainly isn't the self-assured man I walk around with daily. I know the voice is some very young boy lurking deep in the inner recesses of my mind.

I get to know him. Find out what he's feeling. Ask him what he needs to make him happy. Attend to his need to assuage the fear of rejection. All of these things are necessary in our move toward self-care. Most importantly, though, self-discussion is about revealing the truth of a situation.

This hidden, psychological character within, sometimes known as the inner child, often brings to the table an eschewed version of the truth. The majority of the time, we operate psychologically on the premise of false facts. In the case of my business associate, for instance, I wrote to my agent and the agent's assistant at the same time. Both had thought the other had answered the phone messages and the emails. Neither had answered, though, until I wrote to just one and inquired.

I spent a week wondering about the fact that my acting agent didn't want me as a client anymore, when I operated on a false premise from the beginning. I reacted to that little boy inside who fears the worst.

I did ask myself a pertinent question at the end of the week: Do I know for certain that my e-mails and phone calls were ignored?

After thinking about it and deliberating, no one can be certain of another person's activities if he or she is not in the presence of what's happening. I came to the decision, that I had no idea if either my agent or her assistant had gotten my e-mails or intentionally ignored them. This led me to write the final e-mail that got an answer.

Persistence and finding truth about any situation is the primary reason we use self-inquiry. When you discover the truth, you lose the *fear of rejection*, which is the primary cause for the PTSD reaction.

If you have someone say to you, "Yes, I didn't answer your phone call because I don't like you anymore," this actually is easier to face than not having the full truth.

If you can convince yourself that the truth is worth

hearing, because it will bring resolution; then you will continue in your discovery of what's real and what isn't until you come to the end of your rejection.

Discovery 46: How Deep Are Your Roots?

The word *roots* brings back a vision of the old television movie series about slavery in America. If you can recall those days in the 1960s and 70s, you wonder just how far the world has come with prejudice and equal rights. We're on the road, but a little too far from the destination for my taste.

I'm a gardener as a hobby. I have about 350 varieties of flowers and herbs in five different beds around the front of my home. Some flowers go deep into the earth, taking time to develop and create a root system that will keep them alive during the hottest months. Other flowers have short, almost veinlike roots that gather moisture from the dew. Then, others have larger roots that remain and grow larger each year. I have one moon flower that I have to dig up the roots every couple of years, just because it will leech the water from the entire flowerbed.

Roots provide nourishment. A flower naturally knows when it is to bloom. If it blossoms in springtime, then it needs shallower roots, because of the vast rain. But if it is to bloom in the heat of the summer, the plant takes time to develop slowly during the spring and sinks deep into the earth to make sure it will have nourishment and water at the end of summer.

Natural atrophy is one of the aspects I notice most. Sometimes a flower just decides it has had enough and dies, even after a year of gorgeous growth. Other times, small seeds gather and spread to rocks and crevices. There, they grow heartily, when I know I couldn't have possibly planned a flower between rocks.

When something dies in my garden, I recognize that there is now room for something new to grow. When some genes of flower won't take root in my garden, I just assume it doesn't want to be there. I don't get bothered with forcing my garden to be exactly the way I plan it. In fact, there is a certain natural beauty about letting flowers just do their thing. I particularly love how the vines grow around the Koi pond and the rocks of the waterfall.

Deep roots require a lot of strength to dig up. Large trees have to be cut down, then the roots drilled out separately because they are so thick and protude far into the earth.

Humans are similar to those larger trees. As we get older, it gets much harder to transplant, trim, and change. Children, on the other hand, have an easier time with the latter. This is the reason why I look forward to twenty years from now, when the vast majority of the population will have been around long enough to abolish deeply rooted prejudices.

> *Sometimes I make a point of uprooting something in my life, just to make it more difficult to get set in my ways.*

Other times, God sends a hardy wind to blow off my roof. Either way, I get it that everything in life is ephemeral. I want to be used to change and not dig my heels in too deeply, like the pine tree in my front yard that must be sixty years old. I don't see it moving anytime soon. But it's sister tree, standing right next to it, died the year before last. It just withered and turned brown in a period of two weeks, as if it were struck by blight, while the remaining tree stood tall and strong.

If any of us actually knew the future and how to prepare for it, we would feel a lot safer in this world where nothing seems to have immovable roots. Today, let's take a moment to see where we might need to wiggle our roots around a little. Maybe we could even trim away some old branches that no longer serve our entire life. You will be the better for it.

Discovery 47: What Does Your Personal Warning Label Say?

You may be concerned about what designer label you are wearing this week. You should be more concerned about your own personal warning label—the message you send with your body language, your demeanor, and your words. You could be sending the following signals to people you want to impress:

- I have a bad time with relationships, so be scared to have one with me!
- I'm too overweight to be pretty or handsome?
- I'm too scared to talk to anyone, DO NOT APPROACH ME!
- I have never been successful at anything, so don't expect much of me.

The list could go on and on and on.

I'm sure, right off the top of your mind, you will know one label you wear for certain. I bet you proudly wear it. Imagine what you would be without that label. Would life feel foreign? Would you be open to change? I am told my label used to be: I am all together and nothing can shake me!

It's easy to remember the day that this label became null and void. (This story may sound familiar, because I have shared it once, but this version comes from a different point of view.) I had been in a relationship for eight years, the day my partner left his e-mail open on his desktop. Things had been rocky for six months, and I was suspicious. So I looked at the titles of the e-mails and saw one that stuck out. The ex-partner I had been with for seven years before that current relationship had sent my partner an e-mail.

I opened it to discover they were having an affair! That day, my perfect world crumbled. I couldn't stop crying. I would get it together long enough to see clients then schedule fifteen minute breaks between to crumble again. Tears seemed to flow endlessly.

It was during this time that friends said that I actually became available to them on a compassionate level. They said that my "label" of having it all together, put them off and made them feel, somehow, that they had to live up to my ideal of perfection.

In other words, my pain changed my label from "I am all together and nothing can shake me!" to "I am as vulnerable as you are. But that's okay. We can help each other through the hard times in life!"

This new trademark is a much better one to wear. Sometimes you just have to thank the circumstances of life for giving you the opportunity to grow into a better person through the hard times. I don't look back with anger anymore. I look behind me with pride that I was able to sustain a wonderful relationship for eight years that really satisfied my heart and soul. Perhaps, not all relationships are meant to go the distance. That is not for me to say.

Since Spirit God is always wanting us to go deeper and to love deeper, we are always going to be about discovering our personal WARNING LABELS. When we do, we should settle into them and ask God to help us learn to love the changes that are always about to happen.

Change is inevitable when you are about looking inward toward a better and deeper spiritual you. Say this prayer: "Come forth, new life! Teach me to be real. Teach me to love with my whole heart. Teach me the lessons of truth, so that I may share them with everyone I meet. Help me discover what I don't know about myself and create the change to make a difference."

Discovery 48: Failure Is an Ugly Word

Honestly, I never thought as myself as someone who failed. I have had some nonstarters, but have created nothing that really was a total flop. I have had a few bad reviews, but nothing that would devastate a career. Today, I just felt like a total failure with this diet. I caved—truly caved. Remember those cookies I was telling you about that I had saved for when I hit my goal? Well, when I went to throw them away, because this is what I would advise any person to do on a diet, I checked to see if anyone was looking and I ate one—frozen. Yes, frozen. It was as hard as a brick and as sweet as heaven itself.

Then I found myself putting the bag of cookies back in the freezer instead of in the waste paper basket where they belonged. (Damn you, Jennifer, for making such amazing oatmeal, chocolate chip cookies.) They were like cocaine. Once I ate one, I went back for two, then three. I finally stopped at five. I'm amazed I didn't chip a tooth from so many frozen cookies.

This day started off way too early with me taking my car in to get the transmission fixed. A friend had to stay overnight to drive me to the service center. I drank some caffeinated tea and was sorry for it the entire day. I never realized what a diuretic tea could do to me. I was in the bathroom almost every thirty minutes urinating. I even had to excuse myself in the middle of sessions, which is not like me at all.

Everything went well, even with exercise until dinner, when I had to pick up my car, and it wasn't ready. The part the service station had ordered for my car was broken. I had to rearrange my schedule and get a rental car for Wednesday. I guess something as menial as a car not being fixed can put one over the dietetic edge.

I used the anxiousness about the car for an excuse to eat and dove into dinner like a man who hadn't been fed in two days. After dinner I didn't stop eating until 10 pm.

Disappointment doesn't begin to let you know how I felt about my progress. *It will only take me two weeks to lose this weight, my ass.* I think a change in behavior is going to take a solid desire to be different—to act in a different way—completely, toward food.

To be a good coach, you don't actually have to be good at the sport. I'm good at helping people lose weight. I have helped 1000s of people get to their goals. My brother-in-law is a tremendous football coach. I can't imagine that he could get his body around the track once today. There are many older ballet coaches who are considered the best in the world, but could never dance again in their lives. The list of coaches who are great at teaching but not so good at doing their craft anymore can go on forever. I guess, for now, I fit in to the latter.

I do know this: I'll keep trying. I'm not a quitter. But I may fall a few more times before I actually make some more progress. Upward and onward.

Weight loss: -.2 total!

Discovery 49: Our Deepest Desire Is...

How many times in your life have you dreamed of sailing on the wind, higher than the trees and the world, carefree and almost weightless? I know that many of my most amazing visions have included flying.

I remember a few dreams that felt as if I were a bird sailing freely through pathways of trees, back into the past, and breezing through the future. Last night, I dreamed I was a winged creature capable of flying quickly and easily through the earthly plane. I awoke feeling amazed, as if I had come out of my body and moved from the form of a caterpillar to a butterfly.

The dream made me wonder if my spirit were allowed to exist primarily outside of this human shell, if I would actually be able to fly. Who knows really? I do recognize that humanity has an innate desire to fly. As soon as mechanical devises existed, inventors tried hard to make one to fly, until the airplane was discovered.

Even before that there were films of people trying to create synthetic wings to jump off of high cliffs, sometimes to their deaths, just to prove that humans could fly. After the airplane, we wanted to sail higher than the world, to reach for the stars and invented rockets that flew to the moon and beyond.

The spiritual practice of meditation is actually meant to liberate you from the constraints of the physical body. We are creatures that seem to feel trapped in our human shell and innately want to move toward our true Self.

In my own imaginings and in many spiritualists' accounts, our spirit is capable of flying, moving through space and time, and has the ability to change shape. If this is true, then during a meditation, we could imagine this blissful space, as we become the observer of the body and enter into a metaphysical state (meta means *out from the body*).

Finding Authentic You

Many have tried to define the parameters of meditation. Buddhists would love to be in the simple silence. Christians and Jews are more apt to reach for meditation as a prayerful place where God and man become one. Other religions use a meditative place for worship.

I believe that meditation is meant to give us wings to fly into a place where power and truth exist. In this place we find the spiritual gift of creation and the honor of being able to make effective change in our lives. What we bring back to the human, physical body in the form of faith could, and should, someday express itself in the physical.

Our entire spiritual walk is moving toward gaining this power of meditation and creativity. This is why our antagonist, the world, is so full of alluring ventures that draw us away from the pure power and peace that actually could give us everything we desire and need to be complete on this Earth. If today you could seek for one thing, what would that be?

I believe that we take turns in our groups of families and friends teaching each other lessons by playing different roles for the purpose of learning. This is why I believe our spirits must reincarnate many times until all of our lessons are learned. This theory helps me see that even though someone is playing the Judas role in my life, he may be the exact blessing I need to help crucify a part of my mind that no longer serves my life.

My sole purpose in life is simply to live it completely and fully—to gain from it every lesson, every joy, and experience I can attain. To be present and in the NOW, I must get the full human experience to move on to the next stage of my spiritual development.

I am now and have always been—God experiencing itself as many, individuated parts of the whole.

Discovery 50: Gateway to Happiness

Every time someone dies in my life, I think of one thing: Why am I wasting so much of my life in homeostasis? Obviously, as you have been reading the dicoveries, I have had a few deaths these past couple years as I have written this book. Death is like pulling a *wake-up* card in your daily reading and stapling it to your forehead. "Hey, you! Life is short. You never know when your time is up! Get with it! Do what you're here to do!"

I've been writing a great deal about our life's purpose. A good reason exists for this. Without a clear vision of your future, you will cease to exist. I'm not saying that you will die physically. I believe you will perish mentally.

You will end up in complacency. Every year of my life, I had created defined dreams for the future, written them in a journal, and seeked to accomplish them in the coming year. I noticed, as I did this, I would achieve almost every goal before the end of the year.

About three years ago, though, I went to the beach. The only goal that kept coming to my mind was:

> *Your journey now is to be 'goal free' for the entire year. Be led by Spirit every day.*

As I tried my best to stay out of my controlling mind—which is really strong—I watched as my level of complacency deepened. I didn't know how to act without a goal.

I am, by nature, goal-oriented. I have always been this way. I set my mind to write ten pages of a book a day, and you better believe those ten pages are done, edited, and printed or the rest of my day is useless.

I remember, even as a child, when I had something important that needed to be accomplished, I would say to myself: "If you finish your book report, then you can go outside and play! Otherwise, you have to stay inside and practice the piano."

It was as if, I got the idea of *parenting myself* at a very young age. As I didn't have a caring father or a mother that lived with me or my five siblings, no one but me existed in my young life to play that role. I just kept thinking, if I'm not brilliant and talented, then I will never get out of this hell hole of a town. I'll end up like everyone else who works at the steel mill and gets cancer from the steel dust in his lungs.

That was enough to get me a 4.0 grade average in high school and surge forth into college on almost a full scholarship to Carnegie Mellon University. No parent helped me do my financial statements for a student loan. No teacher led me along the path of where I wanted to go. I just jumped in and did it. Fear never had a dwelling place when it came to getting things accomplished.

Making life happen is usually about removing the blocks to your creative mind. My friend Sharon has to play the piano, play the organ, clean the kitty litter box, and watch an hour of television before she can get to finishing her Master's Thesis.

I always tell her, "Wouldn't it just be easier to define a time to work and just work? Why do you have to go through this avoidance ritual every time you intend to work?"

Her answer, "I just can't seem to get motivated to do what I know I have to do."

Isn't this most people's answer to life?

> *Today is the day you are going to find the gateway to happiness. You are motivated to take whatever has been troubling you, holding you back, and standing in the way of your success and demolish it with*

your mind.

You are now envisioning the pathway to your success as clear and free. You no longer need to sabotage yourself or your career by playing small in this world.

You are a magnificent piece of God—ready for the world to see, hear, and know!

The End

Epilogue: A Daily Prayer

I am knowing that at any time of the day or night, anywhere in the world, all of the goodness and love of Spirit is dissolving and resolving the negativity rising up in our world to create a better and more positive Universe as we recite this treatment together:

> *I stand at the threshold of divine power, wisdom, and truth. All of the good that I can embody is now mine. I have only to open the portals of my mind and accept that which is ready to express through me.*
>
> *I expect, fully and emphatically, the answer to my prayers for peace in my life and in the world today. I remove my fear of lack and negation, for it is the only barrier that stands in the way of my experience of God's unfloundering love.*
>
> *In this moment perfect good comes to all who pray this prayer—enough and to spare—to give and to share. Love can never be exhausted. Good can never be depleted, because the Source from which it emanates is inexhaustible.*
>
> *Today, in this moment, the Law responds to my thoughts and the thoughts of all people everywhere praying this prayer. My word is one of affirmation, rising from the knowledge that the One Enduring and True God—the Indwelling Essence of Life—reflects perfectly through every soul on Earth now!*

Finding Authentic You

About the Author

Bo Sebastian has had many well-known works published including his most recent self-help guide, *Learning Alone, Finding Authentic You: 7 Steps to Effective Change*. Also, NY Times Bestseller, *Your Gay Friend's Guide to Understanding Men, Uncommon Gay Spiritual Warrior, Theoraphasz: God Speaks*, a collaborative novel, *Summer in Mossy Creek* with Bell Bridge Books and BelleBooks Publishers, and *The Protein-Powered Vegetarian* are all a part of his collection of books. He has a fitness DVD: *Boga Fitness*, merging Yoga with core strength and fitness exercises.

Bo has written five novels: *The Leaving Cellar, Billy Ray's Secret, Marlene and the Religiously Insane, Fatal Virtues*, and a young reader's novel, *Willa Divine, The Princess of Dixon County*.

He has been a Vegetarian Chef to vegetarian dignitaries and a teacher of the vegetarian ways to chefs around the globe. For today's growing need to understand gluten-free recipes, his innovative book: *Gluten-Free, High Protein, Mostly Vegetarian Recipes & Cookbook* will help you easily change your gluten habits to wheat-free habits.

Bo is the author of the world famous blog: FindingAuthenticYou.com and proudly wears the hat of renowned life-, and health-coach in South Florida. For more information about Bo, visit BoSebastian.com.